FAVOURITE GREEK MYTHS

Frontispiece (*overleaf*)
by Denise L. Brown R.E.
This depicts the moment when
Pandora let loose all the troubles of
the world. The container is usually
referred to as *Pandora's Box*, but
it is here more correctly depicted as
a storage-jar.

FAVOURITE GREEK MYTHS

BY

LILIAN STOUGHTON HYDE

Great God! I'd rather be
A Pagan suckled in a creed outworn;
So might I, standing on this pleasant lea,
Have glimpses that would make me less forlorn,
Have sight of Proteus rising from the sea,
Or hear old Triton blow his wreathed horn.

WORDSWORTH

HARRAP LONDON

First published in Great Britain 1905
by GEORGE G. HARRAP & CO. LTD
182 - 184 High Holborn, London WC1V 7AX

Reprinted: 1907; 1908; 1909; 1910; 1912; 1913; 1914;
1915 1917; 1918 (*twice*); 1919; 1922; 1923; 1924;
1925; 1927 (*twice*); 1928; 1929; 1930; 1932; 1933;
1934; 1937; 1939; 1942; 1945; 1947; 1949; 1952;
1953, 1954, 1956
Reset and reprinted 1960
Reprinted: 1961; 1962; 1964; 1967
Second Edition Revised 1973

ISBN 0 245 52001 5 (*Boards, jacketed*)
ISBN 0 245 51998 X (*Boards*)

Printed in Great Britain by
Redwood Press Limited
Trowbridge, Wiltshire

Preface

IN the preparation of this book the aim has been to present in a manner suited to young readers the Greek myths that have been world favourites through the centuries, and that have in some measure exercised a formative influence on literature and the fine arts in many countries. While a knowledge of these myths is undoubtedly necessary to a clear understanding of much in literature and the arts, yet it is not for this reason alone that they have been selected; the myths that have appealed to the poets, the painters, and the sculptors for so many ages are the very ones that have the greatest depth of meaning, and that are the most beautiful and the best worth telling. Moreover, these myths appeal strongly to the child mind, and should be presented while the young imagination can make them live. At first children will enjoy them as stories; but in later years they will see them as the embodiment of spiritual truths.

CONTENTS

Introduction

MANY thousands of years ago there lived a race of people whom we call the Aryans. To this people everything seemed alive. When they looked up into the blue sky, where there were white clouds moving, they fancied that they saw a sea on which ships were sailing. Or, if the clouds were numerous and moved swiftly in one direction, driven by the wind, they believed that they saw cows driven by an invisible herdsman. In their eyes the dark storm-clouds were gigantic birds which flew over the sky carrying worms in their beaks. The lightning flashes were the worms, which these birds sometimes let fall. Or, the lightning was a fish, darting through the sea of cloud; or a spear, or a serpent. The storm-cloud was a dragon.

These people never tired of looking at the sky. They sometimes called the clouds treasure mountains, and the lightning an opening in the rock, which gave a glimpse of the bright treasure within. In time they came to think that the bright blue sky of day was a person, to whom they gave the name Father Dyaus (which means Father Sky), saying, because the sky seemed so high above everything else, that

Father Dyaus ruled over all things. They also called the sun a shining wanderer, the golden-eyed and golden-handed god, and said that the darkness of night was a serpent, slain by their sun-god's arrows.

A time came when many tribes of this Aryan race moved on to other lands. Some of them settled in the land we now call Greece, taking with them their quaint stories of the sky and the clouds, of Father Dyaus, and the herdsman of the cloud-cattle, and the golden-eyed sun-god.

In Greece these stories and others were handed down from one generation to another through thousands of years; and while those who told these stories undoubtedly believed that every word was true, and took great pains to tell them exactly as they had heard them, yet in time the stories changed and grew.

After the Aryan tribes who moved into Greece had lived in that country for a long time, they forgot that Father Dyaus (*Dyaus-pitar*) was the blue sky. Instead of calling him by his old name of Father Dyaus, they called him Father Zeus (*Zeus-pater*), the king and father of gods and men, while other Aryan tribes, who were afterward called Romans, knew him as Jupiter (*Ju-piter*). In the same way these people forgot, in time, that the herdsman who drove the cloud-cattle was the wind; they thought him a real person, or a god, and called him Hermes, or Mercury. In this way the old Greeks (that is, the descendants of the Aryans who had settled in Greece) came to believe in many gods, and it was a long, long time after this before they knew anything about the true God.

As time went on, every little kingdom in Greece had its own version of these old stories, or myths. They were told again and again, in the twilight, by the firesides of the people, and were often sung or chanted in kings' houses to the music of the lyre. In comparatively modern times, but still some thousands of years ago, the poets wrote them down, some writing one version and some another. Many of the books they wrote may still be read to-day.

According to the old Greek myths, Jupiter was the king and father of gods and men. He, with the other gods, lived high up on Mount Olympus, above the clouds. He was by far the strongest of the gods. His weapon was the thunderbolt; for the Greeks believed that the lightning flash was a kind of magic stone, shaped like a spear or an arrow, which Jupiter threw at his enemies, or at wrongdoers among men. The storm-loving eagle was Jupiter's bird, and it carried the thunderbolts in its claw.

Neptune and Pluto were brothers of Jupiter. Neptune ruled the sea, and Pluto was the king of the underworld, a dark, gloomy place where people were supposed to go after death. Juno was Jupiter's queen, and therefore the most powerful of the goddesses.

Minerva was the goddess of wisdom, of war for a right cause, and of the arts of peace. She gave the olive tree to the Greeks, and taught the Greek women how to spin and weave. She was the special protectress and helper of heroes.

Apollo was the god of prophecy, music, and poetry. Later, he was the god of the sun, especially of the light which comes from the sun, while Helios was the god of the sun itself. The rays of sunlight, which might sometimes be seen across a dark cloud, were Apollo's golden arrows. These arrows might bring death to mortals.

Diana was the twin sister of Apollo. Just as Apollo was the god of the light of the sun, she was the goddess of the light of the moon, while Selene, the real moon-goddess, was the goddess of the moon itself. Diana was a huntress who wandered over the mountains, carrying a bow and a quiverful of silver arrows. Her silver arrows, like Apollo's golden ones, were sometimes used to punish the guilty. She wore a crown shaped like the new moon, and her favourite animal was the stag.

Venus was the goddess of love and beauty. She was born from the foam of the sea, and was the most beautiful of all the goddesses. When she went abroad, her chariot was drawn by doves and surrounded by flocks of little singing birds.

Mars was the god of war in a bad sense. He loved fighting and bloodshed for its own sake.

Mercury was the herald and swift-footed messenger of the gods. He was the patron of herdsmen, travellers, and rogues. He wore a winged cap and winged sandals, and carried, as the sign of his office, a golden wand or staff, which had two wings at the top and two golden snakes twined around it. This staff was called the caduceus.

Ceres was the goddess of all that grows out of the earth, and was called the Great Mother.

Besides these great ones, there were others, not so strong and wonderful, who instead of living on Mount Olympus, above the clouds, had their homes in certain quiet places of the earth. These humbler ones were called nymphs, fauns, satyrs, river-gods, and Tritons. The nymphs were everywhere; they haunted the meadows, groves, and mountains, and one of them was sure to be found at the bottom of every spring and fountain; they inhabited the trees; they lived in the sea. Fauns were the followers of Pan, the god of shepherds and other country folk. Like Pan, the fauns had little horns, pointed ears, and legs like a goat. Satyrs were the followers of Bacchus, the god of the vine. They had pointed ears, and little horns among their curls, but otherwise were very much like men. Tritons were said to have the upper part of the body like that of a man and the lower part like that of a fish. They lived in the sea, and could quiet its waters by blowing on their shell-trumpets.

In those days there were no solitary places; even the desert had its giants and its pygmies. That time of which the old myths tell us must have been wonderful indeed.

I

Prometheus

THERE once lived a race of huge giants called Titans. These giants were fierce, turbulent, and lawless— always fighting among themselves and against Jupiter, the king of the gods.

One of the Titans, whose name was Prometheus, was wiser than the rest. He often thought about what would be likely to happen in the future.

One day, Prometheus said to his brother Titans: "What is the use of wasting so much strength? In the end, wisdom and forethought will win. If we are going to fight against the gods, let us choose a leader and stop quarrelling among ourselves."

The Titans answered him by a shower of great rocks and uprooted trees.

Prometheus, after escaping unhurt, said to his younger brother: "Come, Epimetheus, we can do nothing among these Titans. If they keep on, they will tear the earth to pieces. Let us go and help Jupiter to overcome them."

Epimetheus agreed to this, and the two brothers went over to Jupiter, who called the gods together and began a terrible battle. The Titans tore up enormous boulders and cast them at the gods, while Jupiter hurled his thunderbolts and his lightnings in all directions. Soon the sky was a sheet of flame, the sea boiled, the earth trembled, and the forests took fire and began to burn.

At last the gods—partly by the help of the wise counsel of Prometheus—conquered the Titans, took them to the ends of the earth, and imprisoned them in a deep underground cavern. Neptune, the sea-god, made strong bronze gates with heavy bolts and bars, to keep the giants down, while Jupiter sent Briareus and his brothers, three giants with fifty heads and a hundred hands each, to stand guard over them.

All but one of the Titans who had fought against the gods were imprisoned in this cavern. This one who was not shut in with the others was Atlas, whose enormous strength was greater than that of his brothers, while his disposition was less quarrelsome. He was made to stand and hold up the sky on his head and hands.

As the Titans could now make no more trouble, there was comparative peace and quiet on the earth. Nevertheless, Jupiter said that, although the men who remained on the earth were not so strong as the Titans, they were a foolish and wicked race. He declared that he would destroy them—sweep them away, and have done with them, forever.

When their king said this, none of the gods dared to say a word in defence of mankind. But Prometheus, the Titan, who was earth-born himself, and loved these men of the earth, begged Jupiter so earnestly to spare them, that Jupiter consented to do so.

At this time, men lived in dark, gloomy caves. Their friend, Prometheus, taught them to build simple houses, which were much more comfortable than the caves had been. This was a great step forward, but men needed more help yet from the Titan. The beasts in the forests, and the great birds that built their nests on the rocks, were strong; but men were weak. The lion had sharp claws and teeth; the eagle had wings; the turtle had a hard shell; but man, although he stood upright with his face toward the stars, had no weapon with which he could defend himself.

Prometheus said that man should have Jupiter's wonderful flower of fire, which shone so brightly in the sky. So he took a hollow reed, went up to Olympus, stole the red flower of fire, and brought it down to earth in his reed.

After this, all the other creatures were afraid of man, for this red flower had made him stronger than they. Man dug iron out of the earth, and by the help of his new fire made weapons that were sharper than the lion's teeth; he tamed the wild cattle by the fear of it, yoked them together, and taught them how to draw the plough; he sharpened strong stakes, hardening them in its heat, and set them around his house as a defence from his enemies; he did many other things besides with the red flower that Prometheus had made to blossom at the end of the reed.

Jupiter, sitting on his throne, saw with alarm how strong man was becoming. One day he discovered the theft of his shining red flower, and knew that Prometheus was the thief. He was greatly displeased at this act.

"Prometheus loves man too well," said he. "He shall be punished." Then he called his two slaves, Strength and Force, and told them to take Prometheus and bind him fast to a great rock in the lonely Caucasian Mountains. At the same time he ordered Vulcan, the lame smith-god, to rivet the Titan's chains—in a cunning way that only Vulcan knew.

There Prometheus hung on the rock for hundreds of years. The sun shone on him pitilessly, by day— only the kindly night gave him shade. He heard the rushing wings of the sea-gulls, as they came to feed their young who cried from the rocks below. The sea-nymphs floated up to his rock to give him their pity. A vulture, cruel as the king of the gods, came daily and tore him with its claws and beak.

But this frightful punishment did not last forever. Prometheus himself knew that some day he should be set free, and this knowledge made him strong to endure.

At last the time came when Jupiter's throne was in danger, and Prometheus, pitying his enemy, told him a secret which helped him to make everything safe again. After this, Jupiter sent Hercules to shoot the vulture and to break the Titan's chains. So Prometheus was set free.

2

How Troubles came into the World

A VERY long time ago, in the Golden Age, every one was good and happy. It was always spring; the earth was covered with flowers, and only gentle winds blew to set the flowers dancing.

No one had any work to do. People lived on mountain strawberries, which were always to be had for the gathering, and on wild grapes, blackberries, and sweet acorns, which grew plentifully in the oak forests. Rivers flowed with milk and nectar. Even the bees did not need to lay up honey, for it fell in tiny drops from the trees. There was abundance everywhere.

In all the whole world, there was not a sword, nor any weapon by means of which men might fight with one another. No one had ever heard of any such thing. All the iron and the gold were buried deep underground.

Besides, people were never ill; they had no troubles of any kind; and never grew old.

The two brothers, Prometheus and Epimetheus, lived in those wonderful days. After stealing the fire for man, Prometheus, knowing that Jupiter would be angry, decided to go away for a time on a distant journey; but before he went, he warned Epimetheus not to receive any gifts from the gods.

One day, after Prometheus had been gone for some time, Mercury came to the cottage of Epimetheus, leading by the hand a beautiful young woman, whose name was Pandora. She had a wreath of partly opened rosebuds on her head, a number of delicate gold chains twisted lightly around her neck, and wore a filmy veil which fell nearly to the hem of her tunic. Mercury presented her to Epimetheus, saying the gods had sent this gift that he might not be lonesome.

Pandora had such a lovely face that Epimetheus could not help believing that the gods had sent her to him in good faith. So he paid no heed to the warning of Prometheus, but took Pandora into his cottage, and found that the days passed much more quickly and pleasantly when she was with him.

Soon, the gods sent Epimetheus another gift. This was a heavy box, which the satyrs brought to the cottage, with directions that it was not to be opened. Epimetheus let it stand in a corner of his cottage; for by this time he had begun to think that the caution of Prometheus about receiving gifts from the gods was altogether unnecessary.

Often, Epimetheus was away all day, hunting or

fishing or gathering grapes from the wild vines that grew along the river banks. On such days, Pandora had nothing to do but to wonder what was in the mysterious box. One day her curiosity was so great that she lifted the lid a very little way and peeped in. The result was similar to what would have happened had she lifted the cover of a bee-hive. Out rushed a great swarm of little winged creatures, and before Pandora knew what had happened, she was stung. She dropped the lid and ran out of the cottage, screaming. Epimetheus, who was just coming in at the door, was well stung, too.

The little winged creatures that Pandora had let out of the box were Troubles, the first that had ever been seen in the world. They soon flew about and spread themselves everywhere, pinching and stinging whenever they got the chance.

After this, people began to have headaches, rheumatism, and other illnesses; and instead of being always kind and pleasant to one another, as they had been before the Troubles were let out of the box, they became unfriendly and quarrelsome. They began to grow old, too.

Nor was it always spring any longer. The fresh young grasses that had clothed all the hillsides, and the gay-coloured flowers that had given Epimetheus and Pandora so much pleasure, were scorched by hot summer suns, and bitten by the frosts of autumn.

Oh, it was a sad thing for the world, when all those wicked little Troubles were let loose!

All the Troubles escaped from the box, but when Pandora let the lid fall so hastily, she shut in one little winged creature, a kind of good fairy whose name was Hope. This little Hope persuaded Pandora to let her out. As soon as she was free, she flew about in the world, undoing all the evil that the Troubles had done, that is, as fast as one good fairy could undo the evil work of such a swarm. No matter what evil thing had happened to poor mortals, she always found some way to comfort them. She fanned aching heads with her gossamer wings; she brought back the colour to pale cheeks; and, best of all, she whispered to those who were growing old that they should one day be young again.

So this is the way that Troubles came into the world, but we must not forget that Hope came with them.

3

The Great Deluge

AFTER the Golden Age there came a time when men began to quarrel with one another. Then the gods sent hot summers and cold winters. Men made themselves places in which to live, in caves and grottos, where they might be protected from the hot sun in summer, and from cold winds in winter. They ploughed the ground and grew grain, which they laid away for food during the cold season.

As the world grew older, men became more and more quarrelsome. At last they dug gold out of the ground, where it had lain for so long a time; and they dug out iron too. They quarrelled more sadly than ever over the possession of the bright yellow gold they had found; and, what was worst of all, they made sharp knives and other weapons out of iron, and fought fiercely with each other.

After this, robbery, murder, and many other crimes were common on the earth. Things grew worse and worse, till a man's life was not safe anywhere. Finally, in all the whole world there were only two people who continued to sacrifice to the gods.

These two were Deucalion and Pyrrha, who were good and gentle, like the people who had lived in the Golden Age.

Jupiter, the father of the gods, looking down from Mount Olympus and seeing how wicked the people of the earth had grown, made up his mind that he would destroy them all. So he shut up the North Wind in the caves of Æolus, and sent forth the South Wind, for the South Wind was the wind that would bring the rain.

Clouds gathered over all the earth, and great drops of rain began to fall, slowly at first, then faster and faster. It rained till the grain was laid flat in the fields; still the clouds did not lighten, nor the rain cease falling. The rivers overflowed their banks, and rushed in over the plains, uprooting great trees, and carrying away houses and cattle and men. The sea, as well as the rivers, flowed in over the land, till dolphins played among the branches of forest trees. Sea-nymphs, too, might have been seen peeping out from among great oaks. Still the rain never stopped, and the water rose higher and higher.

Men and animals made their way to the hills as well as they could, wolves, lions, and tigers swimming side by side with sheep or cattle, all in one common danger. They made their way first to the hills and then to the mountains, but the water came creeping up, up, till all but the tops of the highest mountains were out of sight. At last, when the rain stopped, and the clouds broke away a little, only the top of Mount Parnassus, which was the highest mountain of all, remained above water.

Deucalion and Pyrrha were sailing in a little ship, which they had managed to keep afloat. When they saw that the top of Mount Parnassus was still out of water, they anchored their ship there, and sacrificed to the gods.

Now, as you know, Deucalion and Pyrrha had not become wicked like the rest of mankind. When Jupiter saw that only these two were left, he sent out the North Wind to blow away the clouds. Then Neptune, the god of the sea, sent his chief Triton, to blow a long, twisted horn, and the sea heard, and went back to the place where it rightfully belonged.

As the waters rapidly fell away, the earth appeared again, but what a change! Everything was covered with a dismal coating of yellow mud. And it was so very still—not a sound from any living thing! Deucalion and Pyrrha felt as if even the sound of quarrelling would be better than such perfect silence.

Near by, with its fires out, and covered with mud, was the temple of one of the gods. Deucalion and Pyrrha felt a sense of companionship in its familiar porch, so they went and sat there in the shade, wondering what would become of them—they two, alone in such a great world.

Then a mysterious voice told them to throw the bones of their great mother behind them. It sounded like a friendly voice, but neither Deucalion nor Pyrrha could imagine what was meant by "the bones of their great mother." After they had puzzled over it for some time, they came to the conclusion that their "great mother" must mean Mother Earth, and that her "bones" must be the stones that lay around them. So, standing with their faces toward the temple, they threw the stones behind them. When they turned to see what had happened, they found that the stones which they had thrown had changed into men and women.

In this way, after the Great Deluge, the earth was peopled again; but it is to be feared that some of the people of this new race had hearts as hard as the stones from which they were made.

4

Apollo and Daphne

ONE day Cupid, the little god of love, sat on the bank of a river, playing with his arrows. The arrows were very tiny. Some had points of gold, and others had points of lead. None of them looked as if they could do much harm.

That day Apollo, the great sun-god, walked along the bank of the same river, when returning from his fight with the serpent of darkness, called the Python. He had just used a great number of his wonderful golden arrows in killing this gigantic serpent. Feeling very proud of his victory over the Python, he said, when he saw Cupid at his play, "Ho! What are such little arrows as these good for?" Cupid's feelings were very much hurt at this. He said nothing, but he took his little arrows and flew to the top of Mount Parnassus.

There he sat down on the grass and took a leaden-pointed arrow from his quiver. Looking all about him for some mark for his arrow, he saw Daphne walking through a grove. Daphne was the daughter of Peneus, the river-god. She was so beautiful that the sleeping flowers lifted their heads and burst into full bloom at her coming. Cupid shot the leaden-pointed arrow straight at Daphne's heart. Although it did her no other harm, this little blunt arrow made Daphne feel afraid, and without knowing what she was running away from, she began to run.

Then Cupid, who was very naughty, took a golden-pointed arrow from his quiver, and with this wounded Apollo. The golden-pointed arrow had the power to make Apollo love the first thing he saw. This chanced to be Daphne, the river-nymph, who came running by just then, with her golden hair floating out behind her.

Apollo called to Daphne that there was nothing to fear; then, as she would not stop running, he ran after her. The faster Apollo followed the faster Daphne ran, and she grew more and more afraid all the time, for the little leaden-pointed arrow was sticking in her heart.

She ran till she came to the bank of her father's river, and by this time she was so tired that she could run no farther. She called on her father for help. The river-god heard, and before Apollo could overtake her, changed her into a tree, a beautiful tree with glossy evergreen leaves and blossoms as pink as Daphne's own cheeks.

When Apollo came up with Daphne there she stood, on the bank of the river, not a nymph any longer, but a beautiful tree. Apollo was broken-hearted, at first, to see how he had lost Daphne. It was all the fault of the little golden-pointed arrow. Since this tree was all that was left of Daphne, Apollo loved the tree, and said that it should be planted by the side of his temple. He made himself a crown from its evergreen leaves, which he always wore for Daphne's sake. This tree still grows in Greece, and is called the Laurel of Apollo.

5

How Apollo got his Lyre

MERCURY was the child of Maia, the eldest of the Pleiades, and lived with his mother in a cave among the mountains. One day, when he was only just big enough to walk, he ran out of doors to play in the sunshine, and saw a spotted tortoise-shell lying in the grass. He laughed with pleasure at sight of the pretty thing, and quickly carried it into the cave. Then he bored holes in the edge of the shell, fastened hollow reeds inside, and with a piece of leather and strings made a lyre of it. This was the first lyre that was ever made, and most wonderful music lay hidden in it.

That night, when his mother was asleep, Mercury crept slyly out of his cradle and went out into the moonlight; he ran to the pastures where Apollo's white cattle were sleeping, and stole fifty of the finest heifers. Then he threw his baby-shoes into the ocean, and bound great limbs of tamarisk to his feet, so that no one would be able to tell who had been walking in the soft sand. After this, he drove the cattle hither and thither in great glee for a while, and then took

them down the mountain and shut them into a cave—
but one would think from the tracks left in the sand
that the cattle had been driven up, instead of down
the mountain.

A peasant, who was hoeing in his vineyard by the
light of the full moon, saw this wonderful baby pass
by, driving the cattle, and could hardly believe his
own eyes. No one else saw Mercury; and just at
sunrise, the little mischief went home to his mother's
cave, slipped in through the keyhole, and in a twinkling was in his cradle with his tortoise-shell lyre held
tightly in his arms, looking as if he had been sleeping
there all night.

Apollo soon missed his cattle. It happened that the
man who had been hoeing his grape-vines by moonlight was still working in the same field. When Apollo
asked him whether he had seen any one driving
cattle over that road, the man described the baby
that he had seen, with the curious shoes, and told
him how it had driven the cattle backward and
forward, and up and down.

By daylight, the road looked as if the wind had been
playing havoc with the young evergreens. Their
twigs were scattered here and there, and great
branches seemed to have been broken off and blown
about in the sand. There were no tracks of any living
thing, except the tracks of the cattle, which led in all
directions. This was very confusing, but Apollo,

knowing that no baby, except his own baby brother, could drive cattle, went straight to Maia's cave.

There lay Mercury in his cradle, fast asleep. When Apollo accused him of stealing his white cattle, he sat up and rubbed his eyes, and said innocently that he did not know what cattle were; he had just heard the word for the first time. But Apollo was angry, and insisted that the baby should go with him to Jupiter, to have the dispute settled.

When the two brothers came before Jupiter's throne, Mercury kept on saying that he had never seen any cattle and did not know what they were; but as he said so, he gave Jupiter such a roguish wink that he made the god laugh heartily. Then he suddenly caught up his lyre, and began to play. The music was so beautiful that all the gods in Olympus held their breath to listen. Even Jupiter's fierce eagle nodded his head to the measures. When Mercury stopped playing, Apollo declared that such music was well worth the fifty cattle, and agreed to say no more about the theft. This so pleased Mercury that he gave Apollo the lyre.

Then Apollo, in return for the gift of the wonderful lyre, gave Mercury a golden wand, called the caduceus, which had power over sleep and dreams, and wealth and happiness. At a later time two wings fluttered from the top of his wand, and two golden snakes were twined round it. Besides presenting

Mercury with the caduceus, Apollo made him herdsman of the wonderful white cattle. Mercury now
drove the fifty heifers back to their pastures. So the
quarrel was made up, and the two brothers, Apollo
and Mercury, became the best of friends.

On a day when the wind is blowing and driving
fleecy white clouds before it, perhaps, if you look up,
you will see the white cattle of Apollo. But you will
have to look very sharp to see the herdsman, Mercury.

6

Mercury and Argus

ARGUS was a watchman with a hundred eyes, set
in a circle all around his head. When he slept, he
closed only two eyes at a time; the other ninety-eight
were always wide open. So it could not have been
easy to steal away anything that Argus was watching.

Now it happened that Juno, the wife of Jupiter,
was very jealous of a beautiful river-nymph, called
Io. Jupiter, in order to save Io from the jealous anger
of Juno, changed her into a white heifer. Juno, suspecting that the white heifer was really Io, set Argus
with his hundred eyes to watch her.

Poor Io was very unhappy. Her father, the river-
god, did not know her, neither did her sister-nymphs;
but they used to pat the heifer and give it grass from
their hands. At last Io wrote her name with her hoof
in the sands of the river bank, and then her father
and sisters knew that the pretty white heifer was
their own Io.

She had no sooner revealed herself to her family
in this way than Argus drove her away to a field that
lay far back from the river, where the river-god and

the nymphs could not come, and then set himself
down on the top of a high hill, meaning to watch her
more closely than ever.

Jupiter felt sorry for Io, still he did not dare change
her back into her natural form while Argus was
watching her. But remembering how Mercury, when
he was less than a day old, had stolen away the cattle
of Apollo, he now set this prince of thieves, this
mischief-loving Mercury, to steal Io away from
Argus.

Mercury thought there could be no better fun.
He laid aside his winged cap and his winged shoes,
and dressed like the shepherds in that country. He
carried his golden wand, the caduceus, in his hand,
and as he walked along, played carelessly on a
shepherd's pipe; then, finding a few goats feeding at
the side of the road, he drove them slowly before him.

Argus found his watch rather tiresome, and was
glad enough to talk to any one who happened to pass
by. He was very glad when he saw Mercury coming
with the goats, and he invited the pretended shepherd
to come and sit by him, under the trees in the shade,
and play on his pipe and tell stories.

Mercury sat down on a stone by the side of Argus,
and began to play—very softly, so softly that the
music was like the sighing of the wind through the
branches of the trees. The day was warm, and there
was no other sound except the shrill singing of the

cicadas. Two of Argus's eyes soon closed. The others might have remained open if there had not been a drowsy magic in Mercury's piping. The soft notes came soothingly, slower and slower, and one after another Argus's other eyes began to close, till only two remained open. These two eyes were very bright; they fairly twinkled, and they kept their watch on Io through all Mercury's playing. Then Mercury began to tell stories, and at last the two twinkling eyes closed, like the others. Argus, with all his hundred eyes, was fast asleep. To make him sleep more heavily, Mercury just touched him lightly with the dream-giving caduceus, and then he triumphantly led Io away.

Juno was very angry when she found that her wonderful watchman had slept at his post, slept with all his eyes at once. She said he did not deserve to have so many eyes, if he could not keep some of them open. So she took all of his hundred eyes away from him, and set them in the tail of her pet peacock, who was very proud to wear them. Ever since that day all peacocks have had eyes in their tails.

7

Ceres and Proserpine

I

THE MOURNING OF THE EARTH-MOTHER

IN the island of Sicily, high up among the mountains, there was once a beautiful valley, called the valley of Enna. It was seldom that a human being, even a shepherd, climbed so high; but the goats, being able to climb by the steepest and most slippery paths, over the roughest rocks, knew well what soft, sweet grass grew there. Sheep, too, and sometimes wild swine, found their way to this spot.

Not another mountain valley anywhere was quite like this one. It was never visited by any of the winds except Zephyrus, who was always mild and gentle. The grass was always green and the flowers were always in bloom. There were shady groves on every side, and numberless fountains of sparkling water. It would have been hard to find a pleasanter spot.

This valley of Enna was the home of Ceres, the Earth-mother, one of the wisest of the goddesses. In fact, the valley owed its beauty to the presence of

Ceres, and the wonderful vegetation which covered the whole island of Sicily was due to her influence; for she was the goddess of all that grows out of the earth, and knew the secret of the springing wheat and the ripening fruits. She watched over the flowers, the lambs in the fields, and the young children. The springs of water, too, which came from hidden places of the earth, were hers.

One day Proserpine, the little daughter of Ceres, was playing in the meadows of Enna. Her hair was as yellow as gold, and her cheeks had the delicate pink of an apple blossom. She seemed like a flower among the other flowers of the valley.

She, and the daughters of the valley-nymphs, who were children of about her own age, had taken off their sandals and were running about on the soft grass in their bare feet. They were as light-hearted as the little lambs and kids. Soon they began to gather the flowers that grew so thick on every side—violets, hyacinths, lilies, and big purple irises. They filled their baskets, and then their dresses, and twisted long sprays of wild roses around their shoulders.

Suddenly, Proserpine saw a flower which made her forget everything else. This flower seemed to be a strange, new kind of narcissus. It was of gigantic size, and its one flower-stalk held at least a hundred blossoms. Its fragrance was so powerful that it filled the entire island, and might be noticed even out at sea.

Proserpine called to her playmates to come and see this wonderful flower, and then she noticed, for the first time, that she was alone; for she had wandered from one flower to another till she had left the other children far behind. Running quickly forward to pick this strange blossom, she saw that its stalk was spotted like a snake, and feared that it might be poisonous. Still, it was far too beautiful a flower to be left by itself in the meadow, and she therefore tried to pluck it. When she found that she could not break the stalk, she made a great effort to pull the whole plant up by the roots.

All at once, the black soil around the plant loosened, and Proserpine heard a rumbling underneath the ground. Then the earth suddenly opened, a great black cavern appeared, and out from its depths sprang four magnificent black horses, drawing a golden chariot. In the chariot sat a king with a crown on his head, but under the crown was the gloomiest face ever seen.

When this strange king saw Proserpine standing there by the flower, too frightened to run away, he checked his horses for an instant and, bending forward, snatched the poor child from the ground and placed her on the seat by his side. Then he whipped up his horses and drove away at a furious rate.

Proserpine, still holding fast to her flowers, screamed for her mother.

Helios, the sun-god, saw how the gloomy-faced king had stolen Proserpine away, and Hecate, who sat near by in her cave, heard the scream and the sound of wheels. No one else had any suspicion of what had happened.

Ceres was far away across the seas in another country, overlooking the gathering in of the harvests. She heard Proserpine's scream, and like a sea-bird when it hears the distressed cry of its young, came rushing home across the water.

She filled the valley with the sound of her calling, but no one answered to the name of Proserpine. The strange flower had disappeared. A few roses lay scattered on the grass, and near them were a child's footprints. Ceres felt sure that these were the traces of Proserpine's little bare feet, but she could not follow them far, because a herd of swine had wandered that way and left a confusion of hoofprints behind them.

Ceres could learn nothing about her daughter from the nymphs. She sent out her own messenger, the big white crane that brings the rain; but although he could fly very swiftly and very far on his strong wings, he brought back no news of Proserpine.

When it grew dark, the goddess lighted two torches at the flaming summit of Mount Ætna, and continued her search. She wandered up and down for nine days and nine nights. On the tenth night, when it was nearly morning, she met Hecate, who was carrying a light in her hand, as if she, too, were looking for something. Hecate told Ceres how she had heard Proserpine scream, and had heard the sound of wheels, but had seen nothing. Then she went with the goddess to ask Helios, the sun-god, whether he had not seen what happened that day, for the sun-god travels around the whole world, and must see everything.

Ceres found Helios sitting in his chariot, ready to drive his horses across the sky. He held the fiery creatures in for a moment, while he told Ceres that Pluto, the king of the underworld, had stolen her daughter and had carried her away to live with him in his dark palace.

When Ceres heard this, she knew that Proserpine was lost to her, and she kept away from the other gods and hid herself in the dark places of the earth. She liked to keep away from the earth's people as well as from the gods, for wherever she went, she was sure to see some happy mother with her children around her, and the sight made her feel very lonely. She sometimes envied the poorest peasants, or even the little bird-mothers in the trees.

One day she sat down by the side of the road, near a well, in the shade of an olive tree. While she was sitting there, the four daughters of Celeus, carrying golden pitchers on their shoulders, came down from their father's palace to draw water. Seeing a sad old woman sitting by the well, they spoke to her in a kindly way. Not wishing them to know that she was a goddess, Ceres told the four young princesses that she had been carried away from her home by pirates, and had escaped from being sold for a slave by running away the instant that the pirate's ship reached the shore.

"I am old, and a stranger to every one here," she said, "but I am not too old to work for my bread. I could keep house, or take care of a young child."

Hearing this, the four sisters ran eagerly back to the palace, and asked permission to bring the strange woman home with them. Their mother told them that they might engage her as nurse for their little brother, Demophoon.

Therefore Ceres became an inmate of the house of Celeus, and the little Demophoon flourished wonderfully under her care.

Ceres soon learned to love the human baby who was her charge, and she wished to make him immortal. She knew only one way of doing this, and that was to bathe him with ambrosia, and then, one night after another, place him in the fire until his mortal parts should be burned away. Every night she did this, without saying a word to any one. Under this treatment Demophoon was growing wonderfully godlike; but one night, his mother being awake very late, and hearing some one moving about, drew the curtains aside a very little, and peeped out. There, before the fire-place, where a great fire was burning, stood the strange nurse, with Demophoon in her arms. The mother watched in silence until she saw Ceres place the child in the fire, then she gave a shriek of alarm.

The shriek broke the spell. Ceres took Demophoon from the fire and laid him on the floor. Then she told the trembling mother that she had meant to make her child immortal, but that now this could not be. He would have to grow old and die like other mortals. Then, throwing off her blue hood, she suddenly lost her aged appearance, and all at once looked very grand and beautiful. Her hair, which fell down over her shoulders, was yellow, like the ripe grain in the fields. Demophoon's mother knew by these signs that her child's nurse must be the great Ceres, but she saw her no more, for the goddess went out into the dark night.

After this Ceres continued her lonely wandering, not caring where she went. One day, as she stooped to drink from a spring, Abas, a freckled boy who stood near, mocked her because she looked sad and old. Suddenly he saw Ceres stand up very straight, with a look that frightened him. Then he felt himself growing smaller and smaller, until he shrunk into a little speckled water-newt, when he made haste to hide himself away under a stone.

Unlike Abas, most of the people whom Ceres met with felt sorry for her. One day, while she was sitting on a stone by the side of a mountain road in Greece, feeling very sorrowful, she heard a childish voice say, "Mother, are you not afraid to stay all alone here on the mountain?"

Ceres looked up, pleased to hear the word "mother," and saw a little peasant girl, standing near two goats that she had driven down from the mountain-pastures.

"No, my child," said she, "I am not afraid."

Just then, out from among the trees came the little girl's father, carrying a bundle of firewood on his shoulder. He invited Ceres to come to his cottage for the night. Ceres at first refused, but finally accepted the invitation.

"You are happier than I," said Ceres, as the three walked toward the cottage. "You have your little daughter with you, but I have lost mine."

"Alas! I have sorrow enough," said the peasant. "I fear that my only son, little Triptolemus, lies dying at home."

"Let us hope that he may yet be cured," said Ceres, and stooping, she gathered a handful of poppies.

Soon they came into the little cottage, where they found the mother beside herself with grief for her boy.

Ceres bent over the child and kissed him softly on

both cheeks. As she did so, the poppies in her hands brushed lightly against his face. Then his groans ceased, and the child fell into a quiet sleep.

In the morning Triptolemus woke strong and well; and when Ceres called her winged dragons and drove away through the clouds, she left a happy and grateful family behind her.

II

THE RETURN OF PROSERPINE

All this time, while Ceres had been mourning for her lost Proserpine, she had neglected to look after the little seeds that lay in the brown earth. The consequence was that these little seeds could not sprout and grow; therefore there was no grain to be ground into flour for bread. Not only the seeds but all growing things missed the care of Mother Ceres. The grass turned brown and withered away, the trees in the olive orchards dropped their leaves, and the little birds all flew away to a distant country. Even the sheep that fed among the water-springs in the valley of Enna grew so thin that it was pitiful to see them.

Jupiter saw that without Ceres, the Great Mother, there could be no life on the earth. In time, all men and animals would die for lack of food. He therefore told Iris to set up her rainbow bridge in the sky, and to go quickly down to the dark cave where Ceres mourned for Proserpine, that she might persuade the goddess to forget her sorrow, and go back to the fields, where she was so much needed.

Iris found Ceres sitting in a corner of her cave, among the shadows, wrapped in dark blue draperies that made her almost invisible. The coming of Iris lighted up every part of the cave and set beautiful colours dancing everywhere, but it did not make Ceres smile.

After this, Jupiter sent the gods, one after another, down to the cave; but none of them could comfort the Earth-mother. She still mourned.

Then Jupiter sent Mercury down into Pluto's kingdom, to see whether he could not persuade that grim king to let Proserpine return to her mother.

When Mercury told his errand to King Pluto, Proserpine jumped up from her throne, all eagerness to see her mother again, and Pluto, seeing how glad she was, could not withhold his consent. So he ordered the black horses and the golden chariot brought out to take her back; but before she sprang to the chariot's seat, he craftily asked her if she would not eat one of the pomegranates that grew in his garden.

Proserpine tasted the fruit, taking just four seeds.

Then the black horses swiftly carried Mercury and herself into the upper world, and straight to the cave where Ceres sat.

What a change! How quickly Ceres ran out of the cave, when she heard her daughter's voice! No more mourning in shadowy places for her, now!

Proserpine told her mother everything—how she had found the wonderful narcissus, how the earth had opened, allowing King Pluto's horses to spring out, and how the dark king had snatched her and carried her away.

"But, my dear child," Ceres anxiously inquired, "have you eaten anything since you have been in the underworld?"

Proserpine confessed that she had eaten the four pomegranate seeds. At that, Ceres beat her breast in despair, and then once more appealed to Jupiter. He said that Proserpine should spend eight months of every year with her mother, but would have to pass the other four—one for each pomegranate seed—in the underworld with Pluto.

So Ceres went back to her beautiful valley of Enna, and to her work in the fields. The little brown seeds that had lain asleep so long sprouted up and grew; the fountains sent up their waters; the brown grass on the hills became green; the olive trees and the grape-vines put out new leaves; the lambs and the kids throve, and skipped about more gaily than ever; and

all the hosts of little birds came back with the crane
of Ceres to lead them.

During the eight months that Proserpine was with
her, Ceres went about again among her peasants,
standing near the men while they were threshing the
grain, helping the women to bake their bread, and
having a care over everything that went on. She did
not forget the peasant family of Greece, in whose
cottage she had been invited to pass the night, and
where she had cured little Triptolemus. She visited
this family again and taught the young Triptolemus
how to plough, to sow, and to reap, like the peasants
of her own Sicily.

The time came when Proserpine was obliged to go
back to King Pluto. Then Ceres went and sat among
the shadows in the cave, as she had done before.

All nature slept for a while; but the peasants had
no fear now, for they knew that Proserpine would
surely come back, and that the great Earth-mother
would then care for her children again.

8

Phaethon

PHAETHON was the child of Helios, the sun-god. One could see the glint of the sun's rays in his bright yellow hair, and feel its warmth in the flash of his eyes. He was so full of life and energy that it was a pleasure to watch him. When he was playing with the other boys in the village, if they threw stones, it was Phaethon who could throw the farthest; if they ran races, Phaethon always reached the goal first; and it was the same in all their other sports.

Although these boys could not beat Phaethon in their games, they could say rude things to him, and one day, because they wished to get the better of him in some way, they all met him with a chorus of taunts and sneering words. Among other things, they said that he was not the child of Helios, and this hurt Phaethon very much, for he had always thought it a glorious thing to feel that the god of the great shining sun was his father.

The next morning, as he lay under a tree, gazing steadfastly at the sun, he thought he could see the sun-god, Helios, driving his golden chariot across the sky. "What a fine thing it would be," he said to himself, "if I, boy as I am, could drive that splendid chariot! Then the boys would believe that I am really the child of the sun-god."

The thought had no sooner entered his head than he set out to go to the country where the sun rises. It was a long journey, but at last he saw the golden palace of the sun-god; and then, as he came nearer, he saw Helios himself, sitting on a throne with a crown on his head, while the Hours and the Days stood around him ready to do his bidding. The crown that Helios wore was the most wonderful crown that was ever seen; it was set thick with precious stones of the most dazzling kind; in fact, these stones were so bright that they cast rays of light all around, and whoever looked at them long was sure to be almost blinded.

Even Phaethon's eyes could not long bear the brightness of the crown, so he stood well back from it and told Helios who he was and what the boys had said. Then he asked if there were not some way by which his playmates could be made to believe that he was really the child of the Sun.

Helios took off his crown, so that Phaethon could come nearer, and then he promised to grant any wish that the boy should make. This was a great favour, and Phaethon would not have received it if he had not been a true child of the Sun.

Phaethon clapped his hands in triumph; for he

thought that now he might have his wish. The Hours were already bringing out the golden chariot of the Sun, and it seemed almost as bright as the crown of Helios. Phaethon asked instantly if he might not drive this chariot for one day.

Helios was troubled at hearing such a wish as this, but he had promised, and the gods could not break their promises; accordingly, when the Hours brought out the horses, and made everything ready, he was obliged to let Phaethon take the reins.

The horses of the Sun were powerful animals, as fiery in their temper as any creature that ever lived, even in those days of fire-breathing bulls and dragons. They seemed to be made of fire inside, and they reared and plunged and champed their bits in a way that would have thoroughly frightened most boys. But Phaethon, remembering that he was a child of the Sun, gladly took his place in the chariot.

The four horses started off at a gallop, and Phaethon was so light that the chariot was tossed back and forth as if it had been empty. The horses were frightened at once. They left the right path round the world, and began to run wildly, swerving first one way and then another.

Phaethon saw now, when it was too late, that he was too young to drive such horses. They grew more and more excited, and sparks of fire began to fly from their nostrils. The chariot, too, as it was carried faster and faster through space, began to grow brighter and hotter.

As the horses and chariot came close to the earth, mountain tops took fire and began to smoke. They came closer yet, rivers were dried up, and many, many miles of forest-land and green meadows were scorched and became like a desert. In some countries, too, the heat was so great that the people of those countries were turned to a dark colour. It looked as if the whole world might be burned up.

By this time Phaethon was terrified indeed, for his own hair was on fire. But he did not know what to do.

Jupiter, looking down from Mount Olympus, saw that the world was in great danger. Then suddenly came a terrible clap of thunder, and Phaethon fell from the chariot, down, straight down, like a falling star, into the broad river Eridanus.

And so poor Phaethon, though a true child of the Sun, failed in trying to drive his father's fiery chariot. Perhaps he would never have attempted so daring a deed, had it not been for the unkind taunts of his playfellows. There are some things which even the children of the Sun cannot do.

His sisters, the Heliades, wept for him on the banks of the Eridanus, till at last they were changed into larch trees; and their tears, continuing to fall into the water from the branches of the trees, became drops of clear amber.

9

Clytie

CLYTIE and her sister, Leucothea, were water-nymphs. Early every morning they used to come up from the depths of their river, with other nymphs from neighbouring streams and fountains, and dance among the water-plants on its shores. But with the first rays of the rising sun, all the dancers plunged back into the water and disappeared; for that was the law among water-nymphs.

One morning Clytie and Leucothea broke this law. When the sun began to show above the hills, and all the other nymphs rushed back to their streams, these two sat on the bank of their river, and watched for the coming of the sun-god. Then as Helios drove his horses across the sky, they sat and watched him all day long.

They thought they had never seen anything so glorious. The god sat in his golden chariot with his crown on his head, and kept a firm rein on the four fire-breathing horses. The sisters were dazzled by the glitter of the chariot and the radiance of the jewelled crown. Helios smiled upon them, and they were happy.

When night came, they returned to their river, where they could think of nothing else but Helios and his golden chariot.

Before morning they fell to quarrelling, as sisters sometimes will. Then Clytie told King Oceanus how Leucothea had broken the law of the water-nymphs, but she did not say that she herself had broken it also. King Oceanus was very angry, and shut Leucothea up in a cave.

Just before daylight, Clytie went up to dance with the other nymphs, as usual, and once more she remained on the shore all day to watch the Sun. This time Helios would not smile upon her, because he knew she had been unkind to her sister. When night came, she did not go down to her home at the bottom of the river, but sat on its sandy bank, waiting for the coming of the Sun; and when he came again, she watched him, all day, and so on for nine days and nine nights. As she had broken the law, she did not dare to go home, therefore she had nothing to live on but the dew which fell from the sky. She grew so very thin that you would have thought the wind might blow her away. Foolish Clytie!

Yet, she sat there and watched the Sun, who never looked her way, and never smiled on her any more. At last her dainty feet, that had danced so lightly with the other nymphs, took root in the loose sand;

her fluttering garments became green leaves; and her face, which was always turned toward the Sun, became a flower.

This flower still grows, in wet, sandy places, and still it turns slowly on its stem, always keeping its face toward the sun.

10

The Seven Sisters

AMONG the nymphs of Diana's train were seven sisters, the daughters of Atlas. On moonlight nights these sisters used to dance in the forest glades; and one night Orion, the hunter, saw them dimly through the trees. They looked like a flock of beautiful wild birds, and the sight made the hunter's heart beat loud and fast. Just as he had chased the deer so many times, he began now to chase these nymphs. Not that he meant to hurt them, but he wanted to go near enough to them to see them better. The nymphs were frightened and ran away swiftly through the trees. The faster they ran, the faster Orion followed.

At last the poor frightened sisters came out into an open place, where it was almost as light as day, and there Orion nearly overtook them. Seeing how near he was, the sisters called to Diana for help; and then, when they were almost in the hunter's grasp, they suddenly disappeared, and seven white pigeons rose from the grass where they had been, and flew away—up, up, into the night sky.

When they reached the sky, the seven pigeons became seven bright stars. There the stars shone, in a little group, close together, for hundreds of years. They were called the Pleiades.

Long after the time when the frightened nymphs were changed first into pigeons, and then into stars, one of the sisters left her place among the Pleiades, that she might not see the fall of Troy. While this city was burning, she rushed madly through space, her hair flying out behind her, and men called her a comet. She never returned to her place among the Pleiades.

At the end of his life on earth, Orion too was placed among the stars. He is there, in the sky, to this day, with his lion's skin, his club, and his jewelled belt. Some people say that the Pleiades still fly from before him.

II

Endymion's Sleep

WHEN the plains below were parched and brown and dusty with the heat of summer, on Mount Latmus all was so still and cool, so fresh and green, that one seemed to be in another world. The mountain was most beautiful of all at night, when the moon drove her chariot overhead, and flooded every tree and all the grassy slopes with her pale light.

Endymion was a young shepherd who led his flocks high up on the sides of this mountain and let them browse on the rich pasturage along the margins of its snow-fed streams. He loved the pure mountain air, and the stillness of the higher slopes, which was broken only by the tinkle of his sheep-bells, or the song of birds. There he dreamed his days away, while his sheep and goats were feeding; or, at night, he leaned his head on a log or a mossy stone and slept with the flock.

Selene, the moon-goddess, loved to visit Mount Latmus; in fact, the mountain belonged, in some sense, to her. It was her influence that made everything there so quiet and beautiful. One night, when she had stolen down from her place in the sky for a walk through one of the flowery meadows of Mount Latmus, she found Endymion there asleep.

The shepherd looked as beautiful as any flower on the mountain, or as the swans which were floating on the lake near by, with their heads tucked under their wings. If it had not been for his regular breathing, Selene would have believed that she stood looking at a marble statue. There, at a little distance, lay his sheep and goats, unguarded, and liable to be attacked by wild beasts. Oh, Endymion was a very careless shepherd! That was the effect of the air on Mount Latmus.

Selene knew that it was the wonderful air of her mountain which had made the shepherd heedless, as well as beautiful, therefore she stayed by his flock all night and watched it herself.

She came the next night and the next, and for many nights, to gaze at the sleeper, and to watch the unguarded flock. One morning, when she returned to the sky, she looked so pale from her watching that Jupiter asked her where she had been, and she described the beautiful shepherd she had found on her mountain, and confessed that she had been guarding his sheep.

Then she begged of Jupiter that since Endymion was so very, very beautiful he might always look as she had seen him in his sleep, instead of growing old as other mortals must. Jupiter answered, "Even the gods cannot give to mortals everlasting youth and beauty without giving them also everlasting sleep; but Endymion shall sleep forever and be forever young."

So there, in a cave, on Mount Latmus, Endymion sleeps on to this day; and his wonderful beauty has not faded in the smallest degree, but is a joy still to all who can climb those lofty heights.

12

Why Cadmus founded a City

I

THE LOSS OF EUROPA

ONE day, a little girl called Europa was playing in a meadow by the seashore. She sat on the grass with her lap full of flowers, and was plaiting the flowers into wreaths for her three big brothers, Cadmus, Phœnix, and Cilix, who were not far away.

Suddenly she looked up and saw a snow-white bull, with beautiful silvery horns, standing near her. At first she was afraid, but the bull seemed so gentle, and looked at her in such a friendly way, that she lost all fear of it. Taking some clover blossoms from her lap, she ran up to it and held them to its mouth. It ate the flowers daintily from her fingers, and then began skipping around on the grass almost as lightly as a bird. Finally, coming to the place where Europa was plaiting her flowers, it lay down by her side. She patted it and threw some of the wreaths over its horns, then clapped her hands to see how pretty they looked. After this, she climbed up to its back, when it got up and galloped around the meadow with her. Europa, holding on by one of its white horns, laughed, and enjoyed the ride, and did not notice that the bull was taking her farther and farther away from home, and closer to the shore, till it suddenly jumped into the sea and began to swim away with her. Then she was frightened and screamed for her brothers, who heard her, and ran down to the shore. But they could not stop the white bull. Europa was carried off, and was never seen nor heard from again.

When the three brothers told their father, King Agenor, what had happened, he was quite broken-hearted and very angry besides. He said that little Europa should not have been left alone, and he blamed Cadmus more than the other brothers, because Cadmus was the oldest.

Finally he said to Cadmus, "Go and find Europa and bring her back; or, if you cannot find her, never enter the doors of your father's palace again."

In those days, one could not go far from a walled city without meeting with many dangers; hence, in order that Cadmus might not be entirely alone, his father sent two slaves to bear him company.

When the great gates of the city closed behind them, the three started out, walking toward the west, as that was the direction that the bull had taken. They passed through lonely forests; they crossed mountain-chains; they contrived to make their way across the sea to other lands; but they could not find Europa nor hear any news of her. Cadmus felt quite sure that the search was useless.

II

CADMUS AND THE DRAGON

As Cadmus did not dare to go home without his sister, he asked the oracle at the shrine of Apollo what he should do. The shrine of Apollo was in a cave at the foot of Mount Parnassus, and the oracle was a mysterious voice that seemed to come from the heart of the mountain. The voice told Cadmus to follow a white heifer he would see, and afterward to build a city on the spot where he saw her lie down.

After leaving the cave, Cadmus hardly had time to scramble down into the road again before he saw a white heifer, which he followed, as the voice had told him to do. When the heifer came to a certain beautiful valley, she raised her head, as if she were looking up to heaven, and then made a great lowing, after which she lay down, seemingly quite contented with the spot. Cadmus knew that this was the place where he must build his city.

Near the spot the heifer had chosen was a grove of very old trees, and among the trees, in a rocky place,

was a cave. The mouth of the cave was so choked
with willows that one could not see what it was like
inside, but Cadmus thought he could hear water
trickling down, and the sound seemed so cool and
inviting that he sent one of his slaves into the cave
to look for a spring. The man did not come back.
Then Cadmus sent the other slave to see what had
become of the first one. But that one did not come
back either.

So Cadmus threw a lion's skin around his shoulders, took his lance and his javelin, and went into
the mouth of the cave himself. At first, it was so dark
inside that he could see nothing. When his eyes had
become accustomed to the change from the bright
sunshine he had just left, he saw, in the darkness,
two bright spots, and knew that they must be the
two eyes of some beast. As he could see better, he
made out the form of a huge dragon lying with one
of its ugly claws across something, which he feared
might be the body of one of his faithful slaves. He
took up a large stone and hurled it straight at the
creature's head, but the scales of the dragon were so
hard and tough that the stone rolled away without
doing it any harm. Then he threw his javelin at it,
and wounded it with that; but not being much
disabled, the creature came out of the cave hissing,
and attacked him fiercely. As it came nearer, he
pushed his lance straight into its open mouth, and

finally pinned it to an oak which grew there, and so killed it.

As Cadmus stood looking at the dragon, he realized that although he had killed the monster, he had lost his two slaves, and was alone in a strange country, where, without help, he would have to build the city ordered by the oracle. Just then he was aware that some one was standing at his side. He looked up and saw a tall, strong-looking woman with clear gray eyes. She had a lance in her hand and a helmet on her head. He knew at once that it was the warrior-goddess, Minerva, and as he looked at her he felt his courage coming back.

Minerva told him to plough the ground near by and sow the dragon's teeth. This seemed like strange seed to plant, but Cadmus did as he was bidden to do, and then stood waiting to see what would happen. After a short time the soil began to heave up a little in places, as it does when corn is growing, then, instead of blades of corn, sharp steel points began to show. As they came up farther, these looked like spear-points; then helmets appeared all along the rows; finally, fully armed men had grown up out of the earth and stood looking around fiercely, ready to fight.

Cadmus thought he had a worse enemy now than the dragon, and made ready to defend himself. But there was no need. For the armed men were hardly out of the soil before they began fighting, one with another, and they fell so fast that soon only five were left.

But these last five were wiser than their brothers, for they saw that they gained nothing by killing one another. Instead, they threw their arms on the ground with a crash, and shook hands, to see what would come from helping others.

This worked much better. Cadmus shook hands with the rest, and then they all united to build the city on the spot where the heifer had lain down. The new city was called Thebes. It was prosperous, and all lived there happily for many years, with Cadmus as king.

13

Echo

ECHO was a nymph who talked too much. She was very fond of having the last word. One day she spoke rudely to the great Juno, who said that for this offence Echo should never use her voice again, unless to repeat what she had just heard, but since she was so very fond of last words, she might repeat the last words of others.

This was almost as bad as if Juno had changed her into a parrot. Echo was very much ashamed, and hid herself in the forest.

Narcissus, a young man who had hair as yellow as gold and eyes as blue as the sky,—a very rare thing in Greece, where most people were very dark,—used to hunt in the forest where Echo was hiding. As she was peeping out shyly from some cave or from behind a great tree, Echo often saw Narcissus, and she admired him very much.

One day Narcissus became separated from his friends, and hearing something rustle among the leaves, he called out, "Who's here?"

"Here," answered Echo.

"Here I am. Come!" said Narcissus.

"I am come," said Echo; and, as she spoke, she came out from among the trees.

When Narcissus saw a stranger, instead of one of his friends as he had expected, he looked surprised and walked quickly away.

After this, Echo never came out and allowed herself to be seen again, and in time she faded away till she became only a voice.

This voice was heard for many, many years in forests and among mountains, particularly in caves. In their solitary walks, hunters often heard it. Sometimes it mocked the barking of their dogs; sometimes it repeated their own last words. It always had a weird and mournful sound, and seemed to make lonely places more lonely still.

14

Narcissus

NARCISSUS had a twin sister whom he loved better
than any one else in the world. This sister died when
she was young and very beautiful. Narcissus missed
her so very much that he wished he might die too.

One day, as he sat on the ground by a spring,
looking absently into the water and thinking of his
lost sister, he saw a face like hers, looking up at him.
It seemed as if his sister had become a water-nymph
and were actually there in the spring, but she would
not speak to him.

Of course the face Narcissus saw was really the
reflection of his own face in the water, but he did not
know that. In those days there were no clear mirrors
like ours; and the idea of one's appearance that could
be got from a polished brass shield, for instance, was
a very dim one. So Narcissus leaned over the water
and looked at the beautiful face so like his sister's,
and wondered what it was and whether he would
ever see his sister again.

After this, he came back to the spring day after
day and looked at the face he saw there, and mourned

for his sister until, at last, the gods felt sorry for him and changed him into a flower.

This flower was the first narcissus. All the flowers of this family, when they grow by the side of a pond or a stream, still bend their beautiful heads and look at the reflection of their own faces in the water.

15

Hyacinthus

HYACINTHUS was a beautiful Greek boy who was greatly loved by Apollo. Apollo often laid aside his golden lyre and his arrows, and came down from Mount Olympus to join Hyacinthus in his boyish occupations. The two were often busy all day long, following the hunting-dogs over the mountains or setting fish nets in the river or playing at various games.

Their favourite exercise was the throwing of the discus. The discus was a heavy metal plate about a foot across, which was thrown somewhat as the quoit is thrown. One day Apollo threw the discus first, and sent it whirling high up among the clouds, for the god had great strength. It came down in a fine, strong curve, and Hyacinthus ran to pick it up. Then, as it fell on the hard earth, the discus bounded up again and struck the boy a cruel blow on his white forehead.

Apollo turned as pale as Hyacinthus, but he could not undo what had been done. He could only hold his friend in his arms, and see his head droop like a lily on a broken stem, while the purple blood from his wound was staining the earth.

There was still one way by which Apollo could make Hyacinthus live, and this was to change him into a flower. So, quickly, before it was too late, he whispered over him certain words the gods knew, and Hyacinthus became a purple flower, a flower of the colour of the blood that had flowed from his forehead. As the flower unfolded, it showed a strange mark on its petals, which looked like the Greek words meaning *woe! woe!*

Apollo never forgot his boy friend; but sang about him to the accompaniment of his wonderful lyre till the name of Hyacinthus was known and loved all over Greece.

16

Perseus

I

PERSEUS AND THE MEDUSA

ACRISIUS, the king of Argos, was once very much frightened by a saying of the oracle of Apollo, at Delphi. This oracle had said that King Acrisius would be killed by his own grandson. Now King Acrisius had only one child, a daughter, Danaë, and to prevent the saying of the oracle from coming true, he caused Danaë to be shut up in a strong, brass tower.

Nevertheless, when the spring came and the power of the sun grew greater, when trees began to put out their young leaves or their fuzzy yellow flowers, and when young lambs were bleating in the fields, the news reached King Acrisius that a golden child had been born in the tower.

The golden child was a beautiful baby with blue eyes, a clear white skin, and golden rings of soft hair, all of which the Greeks thought very wonderful.

King Acrisius was quite beside himself with fright

when he heard this piece of news, and he immediately
commanded that Danaë and her golden child should
be put into a brass-bound chest and allowed to float
out to sea.

So Danaë and her baby drifted slowly out to the
great sea, where they had only gulls and a few smaller
sea-birds for company. The waves rocked the chest
gently, and the golden-haired baby slept in his
mother's arms, and did not know that there was
anything to fear; but Danaë thought of strong winds
and high waves, and of sharks and other great fish
that lived in those waters, and her heart was full of
terror.

The chest drifted all night on a quiet sea. In the
early morning, the tides brought it close to the island
of Seriphus, where it became entangled in a fisherman's nets. Dictys, the fisherman to whom the nets
belonged, when starting out for his day's fishing,
saw the chest and drew it in. He took Danaë and her
baby to his brother Polydectes, who was the king of
that island. King Polydectes was willing that Danaë
should stay on the island, and Danaë was very
thankful for this kindness. She found a good home
there; for Dictys and his wife took her into their
own cottage, and did all they could to make her
comfortable.

When the golden child, which Danaë named
Perseus, grew up, he became a strong, handsome

youth who attracted much attention from the people
everywhere. King Polydectes began to wish that the
brass-bound chest had never floated to the island of
Seriphus. In fact, he took a great dislike to Perseus,
a dislike which became an active hatred. The
stronger and handsomer Perseus grew, and the more
admiration his youthful strength and beauty called
forth, the more King Polydectes hated him. He finally
began to think over plans for getting rid of him
forever.

On a rocky, dreary, barren island which lay in the
midst of the sea, a long way from the island of
Seriphus and from every inhabited country, there
lived three fierce sisters who were called the Gorgons.
These strange sisters had faces like women, but do
not seem to have been like women in any other
respect. They had eagles' wings with glittering
golden feathers, scales of brass and iron, claws of
brass, and great fierce-looking tusks which must have
made a strange appearance with their human faces.
Worst of all, instead of hair, their heads were covered
with venomous snakes, that were always twisting
themselves about, and putting out their forked
tongues, ready to bite anything that came within
reach. The two oldest Gorgons had always been just
such fierce creatures as they were now; but the
youngest, who was called the Medusa, had once been
a beautiful woman who was very proud of her long

black curls. In spite of her beautiful face, this
woman's heart was like the hearts of the Gorgons,
and to punish her for a wicked deed she had done,
the gods changed her curls into writhing vipers, and
made her face so terrible that any one who looked at
it was immediately changed into stone. In all other
respects she became a sister to the Gorgons, and had
to go and live with them. She was the most frightful
one of all, because of her power of changing men into
stone.

Now King Polydectes knew all about the Gorgons,
and he made up his mind that there could be no
better way of getting rid of Perseus than to send him
after the Medusa's head. So one day he called the
young man to him, and told him that he expected to
be married soon to the Princess Hippodamia, and
asked him to bring to the wedding-feast, as his gift,
the head of Medusa. He added that, unless Perseus
brought the head with him, he must never come back
to the island of Seriphus again; and then, to make
matters worse, he shut Danaë up in an underground
dungeon, and said she should not come out till
Perseus brought him the head.

Perseus did not even know where the Island of the
Gorgons was, nor how to find it. He thought it must
be somewhere in the western sea, and as he stood on
the shore, looking off at the place in the west where
the sky came down to meet the water, he suddenly

noticed that two people were standing on the sands by his side. One was a very tall woman who wore a helmet on her head and carried a very bright shield on her arm and a lance in her hand. The other was a young man with wings on his cap and on his sandals, a winged staff in his hand, and a crooked sword that shone like a flame, at his side. Perseus knew that the tall woman was Minerva and the young man Mercury, and that they had come to help him. This was just what he had been expecting, for the gods of Olympus often appeared at just the right time, ready to help those who were brave and determined to do all they could for themselves.

First Minerva told Perseus how to find the Island of the Gorgons. She said that he must ask the Three Gray Women, who were cousins of the Gorgons, and that nobody else in the whole world could give him the necessary information. Next she said that when he had found the Gorgons, he must not touch either of the older ones, because they were immortal, and he must by no means look at the Medusa, lest he be turned into stone. Then she took her own bright shield from her arm, and holding it high above her head, bade Perseus see how the shells and pebbles on the shore were all reflected in it. She said that when he was ready to strike off the Medusa's head, he must look at that terrible face only in this shield, which she would lend to him for that purpose.

Now it was Mercury's turn. He lent Perseus his own crooked sword, a sword so sharp that it would cut through brass or iron or any other hard substance. This was the only sword that would cut through the Gorgon's scales. Then he offered to show Perseus the way to the home of the Three Gray Women, who lived in Twilight Land,—a land lying somewhere among the mists that rose from the sea.

The two immediately set out. They journeyed far to the north till they came to a land of cold and fogs. The farther they went, the thicker the fogs became and the darker it grew. At last, in the dim light, they could faintly see, coming toward them, three very old women. Long gray hair hung over their shoulders; their garments and even their faces were gray; and they groped along in the fog as if they could not see. They seemed to be quarrelling about something. As they came nearer, the quarrel proved to be about the use of their one eye; for they were so very old that they had only one eye and one tooth among the three.

"Be quick, Perseus! Now is your time," said Mercury. "Seize their one eye, and then you can compel them to tell you how to find the Gorgons. They will never tell you of their own free will."

So Perseus seized the eye, and would not give it back till the Gray Women had answered his questions. They said that the only way to find the Island of the

Gorgons was to ask the Hesperides, the daughters of Night. These nymphs were the guardians of the famous golden apples in the Garden of the Hesperides, which lay near the place where the giant Atlas held up the sky.

Then Mercury and Perseus started out again, and this time they went far to the west, over land and sea, till they found the Garden of the Hesperides.

The nymphs of the Garden received Mercury and Perseus in a friendly manner. They said they had been expecting the hero who was to slay the Medusa, and would be glad to help him. They pointed out to Perseus the Island of the Gorgons, already dimly visible on the horizon. Then they brought him a pair of winged sandals which had the power to bear their wearer through the air as fast as Mercury's own; the helmet of darkness, which belonged to Pluto, and made its wearer invisible; and the magic pouch, in which he could safely carry the head of the Medusa. Perseus was now well armed, and ready for his work. With Minerva's bright shield, Mercury's crooked sword, the winged shoes, the helmet of darkness, and the magic pouch, he had not so very much to fear after all even from the terrible Gorgons, and was eager to begin the battle.

Thinking that the Gorgons would be asleep by midnight, he waited until that time, and then flew straight to the Island. As he hovered over it, like a

great golden hawk, he looked into Minerva's shield,
by the light of the full moon, and saw a frightful
sight. There were all three of the Gorgons fast asleep.
Around them was what looked at first like a confusion
of strange brown rocks, but the seeming rocks were
really men and animals that had been changed to
stone by the sight of the Medusa's face.

Keeping his eyes on the shield, Perseus dropped
lightly down, and in a flash he had cut off the
Medusa's head and dropped it into the magic pouch.
Then he sped away on the winged sandals, and it
was well that he had these sandals and Pluto's helmet
to make him invisible; for the remaining Gorgons
woke and sprang after him with a terrible cry. He
could hear the rushing of their gold-feathered wings,
the rattle of their brass claws, and the hissing of the
snakes on their heads. But these sounds and even
their terrible cry soon died away; for the Gorgons
could not follow far a foe they could not see. So
Perseus got safely away with the Medusa's head.

Minerva and Mercury had been near Perseus all
the time, although, since he left the Garden of the
Hesperides, they had not chosen to make themselves
visible to him. Minerva heard the shrill cry of the
Gorgons, and she set it into a musical instrument,
which she made on the spot, of thin-beaten bronze,
taken, no doubt, from the hard scales of the Medusa.
Many people have said that this musical instrument

was the flute, but as Minerva was a war goddess, I am sure that it must have been some kind of a war trumpet, and it probably sounded like our fife. Afterward the goddess set the dreadful head of the Medusa on her shield, or sometimes she wore it on her ægis. But before Perseus returned the shield to Minerva and presented her with Medusa's head, he met with many more adventures.

II

PERSEUS AND ANDROMEDA

When the Gorgon sisters had left off following Perseus, he began to fly more slowly with the golden wings of his sandals, and to look down at the mountains and rivers underneath, to see what country he was passing over. When he saw on the tops of the mountains a pink glow from the coming sun, he knew that it would soon be day.

All at once from a clear sky he heard what seemed like a peal of thunder. As the sound echoed back from a hundred hills, it seemed strangely human, like the sighing groan of some gigantic being. Then he saw what appeared to be a weird-looking mountain, with its top among the clouds; but, on coming nearer, he discovered that what he had taken for a mountain was a huge, clumsy giant, who stood holding up the sky on his head and shoulders. The giant had white hair hanging down around his face, and he seemed very tired with the weight of the sky, which had now become yellow with the sunrise light, and looked like an enormous brass bowl turned upside down. No wonder that the poor old giant groaned with the weight of it! Perseus knew that this must be the giant Atlas, of whom he had often heard.

Atlas was as much interested in Perseus as Perseus was in him. For the nymphs who kept the Garden of the Hesperides, the same who had given Perseus the winged sandals and the magic pouch, were the nieces of Atlas, and had told him all about Perseus. This poor giant, with the great weight of the sky on his shoulders, wished that he might get a glimpse of that wonder-working head so that he could be turned into hard, unfeeling rock. Then, he thought, he could hold up the sky forever and not mind the weight of it.

So when he saw Perseus, he hailed him and asked him if he did not carry the Medusa's head in his pouch. When Perseus said that he did, Atlas asked to see it. Perseus warned the giant that the bare sight of this head would turn any living thing into stone; but when Atlas explained that this was just what he wanted, Perseus held up the head for an instant.

Soon after, on his way to Seriphus, Perseus turned and looked back. Where he had left the giant Atlas, he was sure that he now saw a lofty mountain, with snow at the top and forests on the sides. He began to think that he had been dreaming, and that what he had taken for Atlas was really a mountain all the time.

He next flew over a sandy desert, where the sun shone very hot. Here he began to notice a great number of ugly, venomous snakes crawling in all directions. Then he saw a drop of blood fall from the pouch where he carried the Medusa's head, and as it struck the hot sands it became a snake like the rest he had seen, and went crawling away to find some dark hole. Soon another drop of blood fell, and this, too, became a snake. It was plain, now, where all the snakes had come from. That desert is said to be infested with snakes to this day.

After this he began to come to inhabited countries, and he rose higher and flew more swiftly, for he hoped soon to reach Seriphus and set his mother free.

Now it had happened, not very long before the adventure of Perseus with the Medusa, that in a certain country, ruled over by King Cepheus, the people were greatly frightened by the appearance on their coasts of a terrible sea-monster—a huge, scaly creature, with wings like a dragon and a tail like a fish. It must have been a kind of sea-serpent. When the fisherman's little children were playing on the beach, it used to come rushing in from the sea with a great roar, seize a child in its jaws, and carry it off.

The people had shot at it with their bows and arrows, but the arrows had glanced off from its hard scales and fallen harmlessly into the water. Then they had tried to set a net and catch it in that way; but when the great creature found itself entangled, it bit at the cords with its teeth, and lashed about furiously with its tail, till it broke away and went off with what was left of the net clinging to its back.

When this happened, an old priest stepped forward, out of the crowd by the shore, and said that it was of no use for the people to fight with this sea-monster because, undoubtedly, it had been sent by one of the gods.

King Cepheus had a very beautiful daughter. The queen boasted that this daughter, whose name was Andromeda, was even more beautiful than the Nereids, that is, the daughters of the sea-god Nereus. These daughters of Nereus, of whom there were fifty, lived close by in the sea, where they were sometimes seen driving chariots drawn by dolphins. All were beautiful, and one, Galatea, was famous for her beauty.

So this old priest was sure that Nereus himself had sent this sea-monster, and he said it would never go away unless the king caused Andromeda to be chained to a rock, at the edge of the water, and to be left there until the monster took her for its prey.

These were terrible words for the king and queen

to hear. They attempted to take Andromeda away
and hide her in the palace; but they were prevented
from doing so by the people, who, rushing in
between them and the palace gates, took Andromeda
themselves, bound her with chains, and then fastened
her to a great rock, where at high tide the water
would come in and lap against her feet. There they
left her, and the king and queen did not dare to come
to her rescue.

Andromeda did not know what she had done to
deserve such a cruel fate. As she stood there with her
hands chained, she thought of all the fearful tales
she had heard of the sea-monster, and her face grew
almost as white as the foam that the little waves had
already begun to toss to her feet. She bent her head,
and closed her eyes, to shut out what she feared to
see, and the tears rolled down her cheeks and fell into
the water. Then she heard the sound of wings above
her, and suddenly looked up, expecting some new
danger, but could see nothing whatever. There was a
rush of wings, again, close to her, and something
tapped against the rocks. Then, all at once, she saw,
standing before her, a golden-haired young man, with
a plumed helmet in his hand, gold wings on his
sandals, and a kind of hunting-bag, with something
heavy in it, hung over his shoulder. This of course
was Perseus, but Andromeda thought it must be
some god straight from the sky. When Perseus asked

her why she had been chained to the rock, she gladly told him everything.

In the midst of Andromeda's story, and while Perseus was trying the keen edge of his crooked sword, there was a hoarse roar, and a dashing up of spray, out at sea. Perseus hastily took the heavy Medusa's head from his pouch and laid it on the rocks, covering it carefully with seaweed. Then he spread the wings of his sandals and dashed up among the clouds.

There was another hoarse roar, much nearer now. Soon Andromeda saw the sea-monster coming, holding its great serpent-like head high and ploughing up the water like a war-galley. The next moment Perseus darted down from the sky and hovered over the monster, his sword and shield sparkling in the sun. The creature saw his shadow on the water, and snapped at it savagely. Then straight down Perseus dashed, and before the sea-monster could turn and tear him with its teeth, which were as sharp as knives, he had buried the crooked sword to the hilt in its shoulder. The sea-monster gave a most frightful roar, then turned over on its back, and floated quietly on the water. Andromeda was saved.

When Perseus went back to Andromeda on her rock, he easily cut her chains with his wonderful sword. Then taking up the Medusa's head to put it into the pouch again, he found that the seaweeds with which he had covered it were turned to hard stone, and were as red as the drops of blood which had fallen on them from the Medusa's head. When the Nereids came to play on the shore, they found these strange seaweeds, and scattered the seeds far and wide. Fishermen still believe that the beautiful corals of those coasts came from these seeds.

Meanwhile, the king and queen and all the people had heard the sea-monster's roaring, and had gathered on the shore. When they saw that the monster of which they stood in such terror was really dead, what a cheer they sent up! King Cepheus said that Perseus should marry the Princess Andromeda, and should have the whole kingdom with her.

The people immediately set about making preparations for the wedding-feast. They hung wreaths of flowers on all the houses of the town; they threw perfumes into the open fires; they played on pipes and lyres, and sang and danced to the music. When all was ready, the doors of the royal palace were thrown open and the nobles were invited to the feast.

But there was one noble in King Cepheus's realms who did not rejoice with the rest; this was Phineus, to whom Andromeda had been promised in marriage. He had had nothing to say when Andromeda had been chained to the rock and left to serve as a breakfast for the sea-monster; but now he was ready to defend his rights. So he gathered together all the

armed men he could command, that is, all his
retainers, and while the wedding-feast was going on,
broke into the courts of the palace and then into the
great dining-hall itself. As he entered the hall, he
shouted his war-cry and hurled a lance at Perseus,
but missed his aim. Perseus would have flung back a
heavy bronze bowl which he hastily caught up from
the table, but Phineus ran to the altar for protection.

After this, a general fight began between the king's
men and the followers of Phineus. Lances and javelins
flew back and forth. Andromeda and her mother and
their ladies ran screaming from the room. Phineus's
men, although their cause was so unjust, were getting
the best of the fight. They had Perseus hemmed in,
in a corner, and had driven nearly all the king's men
from the room, when Perseus suddenly shouted,
"If any of my friends are here, let them turn away
their faces." As he spoke, he held up the Medusa's
head, at which Phineus and all his men stiffened into
marble statues, and neither Perseus nor the king had
anything more to fear from them.

King Cepheus would have been glad to have
Perseus stay in Libya, and would willingly have given
him half or even the whole of the kingdom with
Andromeda, as he had said; but Perseus was anxious
to go to Seriphus. So the king fitted out a ship for him,
and sent men to row it. Then all the people gathered on
the shore, and bade Perseus and Andromeda farewell.

III

THE HOME-COMING OF PERSEUS

When the news that Perseus had returned with the head of the Medusa was spread abroad, what a rejoicing there was in the island of Seriphus! King Polydectes alone was not glad. Nevertheless, he pretended to be, and he made a great feast, at which the minstrels sang of the great deeds of Danaë's son. As all the enemies of his mother and himself were gathered together at the feast, Perseus held up the head of the Medusa before them, and so made an end of them, King Polydectes and all. During the absence of Perseus, Danaë had been treated with great cruelty by King Polydectes; but she had one true friend. This was Dictys, the fisherman, the brother of Polydectes. He had done all that he could to help her. Perseus, being now the strongest man in the kingdom, could do as he pleased, therefore he proclaimed Dictys king. Then he took his mother and Andromeda and set sail for Argos, which was his own rightful kingdom. He did not wish to supplant his grandfather, King Acrisius; but he hoped that Acrisius, if he were still living, would have forgotten his fear of the oracle, and would be glad to see the daughter and grandson whom he had sent away in the brass-bound chest so long ago.

By this time the report of all that Perseus had done had spread through the neighbouring kingdoms, and his deeds were told by every fireside. Great enthusiasm prevailed among the people when it was known that the hero was coming among them. Long before the ship of Perseus could reach Argos, Acrisius heard that his grandson was coming home. Instead of being pleased at this news, he was terrified; for he remembered well how the oracle had foretold that he should be killed by his own grandson. He would not even remain in Argos, but went away secretly in the night to the city of Larissa, in Thessaly.

Now it happened that the ship of Perseus, having been blown somewhat out of its course, took him also to Larissa, where he arrived soon after King Acrisius. He found the people of that city celebrating the yearly games, in which, with the permission of King Acrisius, they asked Perseus to join them. King Acrisius did not wish to meet his grandson, but he sat looking on among the spectators. Cheer after cheer went up, as Perseus performed some uncommon feat of strength or skill. King Acrisius could not help feeling proud of his grandson.

To close the games for the day, the young men were throwing the discus. Perseus threw it farther than it had ever been thrown before. To please the people, who were very enthusiastic, he threw it a second time. It flew up higher than ever, in a splendid semicircle, but as it descended, a sudden gust of wind came in from the sea and blew it to one side. It fell among the spectators, struck King Acrisius, and killed him instantly.

Perseus knew by the cries he heard that some one had been killed, and he was very much shocked to find that it was his grandfather, of whose presence in Larissa he knew nothing.

So, in this way, the words of the oracle came true. Perseus reigned in his grandfather's place, in Argos, and was wise and just, and much loved by his people.

17

Arachne

ARACHNE lived in a small village on the shores of the Mediterranean. Her parents were very poor. While her mother was busy cooking the simple meals for the family, or working in the fields, Arachne used to spin all day long.

Her wheel made a steady whirring like the buzzing of some insect. She grew so skilful from constant practice, that the threads she drew out were almost as fine as the mists that rose from the sea near by. The neighbours used to hint, sometimes, that such fine-spun threads were rather useless, and that it might be better if Arachne would help her mother more and spin less.

One day Arachne's father, who was a fisherman, came home with his baskets full of little shell-fish, which were of a bright crimson or purple colour. He thought the colour of the little fish so pretty that he tried the experiment of dyeing Arachne's wools with them. The result was the most vivid hue that had ever been seen in any kind of woven fabric. This was the colour which was afterward called Tyrian purple,—

or sometimes it was called royal purple, because
kings liked to wear it.

After this, Arachne's tapestries always showed
some touch of the new colour. They now found a
ready sale, and, in fact, soon became famous.

Arachne's family changed their little cottage for
a much larger house. Her mother did not have to
work in the fields any more, nor was her father any
longer obliged to go out in his boat to catch fish.

Arachne, herself, became as famous as her tapestries. She heard admiring words on every side, and
I am sorry to say that her head was a little turned by
them. When, as often happened, people praised the
beautiful colour that had been produced by the little
shell-fish, she did not tell how her father had helped
her, but took all the credit to herself.

While she was weaving, a group of people often
stood behind her loom, watching the pictures grow.
One day she overheard some one say that even the
great goddess, Minerva, the patron goddess of spinning and weaving, could not weave more beautiful
tapestries than this plain fisherman's daughter. This
was a very foolish thing to say, but Arachne thought
it was true. She heard another say that Arachne wove
so beautifully that she must have been taught by
Minerva herself.

Now, the truth is, that Minerva had taught
Arachne. It was Minerva who had sent the little

shell-fish to those coasts; and, although she never allowed herself to be seen, she often stood behind the girl and guided her shuttle.

But Arachne, never having seen the goddess, thought she owed everything to herself alone, and began to boast of her skill. One day she said: "It has been said that I can weave quite as well, if not better, than the goddess, Minerva. I should like to have a weaving match with her, and then it would be seen which could do best."

These wicked words had hardly left Arachne's mouth, before she heard the sound of a crutch on the floor. Turning to look behind her, she saw a feeble old woman in a rusty gray cloak. The woman's eyes were as gray as her cloak, and strangely bright and clear for one so old. She leaned heavily on her crutch, and when she spoke, her voice was cracked and weak.

"I am many years older than you," she said. "Take my advice. Ask Minerva's pardon for your ungrateful words. If you are truly sorry, she will forgive you."

Now Arachne had never been very respectful to old persons, particularly when they wore rusty cloaks, and she was very angry at being reproved by this one.

"Don't advise me," she said. "Go and advise your own children. I shall say and do what I please."

At this an angry light came into the old woman's gray eyes; her crutch suddenly changed to a shining lance; she dropped her cloak; and there stood the goddess herself.

Arachne's face grew very red, and then very white, but she would not ask Minerva's pardon, even then. Instead, she said that she was ready for the weaving match.

So two weaving frames were brought in, and attached to one of the beams overhead. Then Minerva and foolish Arachne stood side by side, and each began to weave a piece of tapestry.

As Minerva wove, her tapestry began to show pictures of mortals who had been foolhardy and boastful, like Arachne, and who had been punished by the gods. It was meant for a kindly warning to Arachne.

But Arachne would not heed the warning. She wove into her tapestry pictures representing certain foolish things that the gods of Olympus had done.

This was very disrespectful, and it is no wonder that when Arachne's tapestry was finished, Minerva tore it to pieces.

Arachne was frightened now, but it was too late. Minerva suddenly struck her on the forehead with her shuttle. Then Arachne shrank to a little creature no larger than one's thumb.

"Since you think yourself so very skilful in spinning and weaving," said Minerva, "you shall do nothing else but spin and weave all your life."

Upon this Arachne, in her new shape, ran quickly into the first dark corner she could find. She was now obliged to earn her living by spinning webs of exceeding fineness, in which she caught many flies, just as her father had caught fish in his nets. She was called the Spinner.

The children of this first little spinner have become very numerous; but their old name of *spinner* has been changed to that of *spider*. Their delicate webs, which are as mist-like as any of Arachne's weaving, often cover the grass on a morning when the day is to be fine.

18

Jason and the Golden Fleece

I

THE MAN WITH ONE SANDAL

JASON was the son of King Æson, and heir to his father's kingdom of Iolcus. One day, when Jason was a helpless infant in his cradle, a certain strong chief, called Pelias, came to the palace with a great body of armed men, broke through the gates, entered, and took King Æson captive.

In the midst of all the noise and confusion, Jason's nurse managed to escape with her charge. She ran down a lonely country road, and across the marshes to the mountains, to Chiron's cave.

Chiron was a centaur. Like all centaurs, he had the body and legs of a horse, and the head and shoulders of a man. He lived in a cave, as poor people often did in those days, and he supported himself by keeping a kind of school. His pupils became very expert horsemen, and good musicians. By hunting wild beasts in the forests, they learned the use of the spear, the shield, and other implements of war. Chiron's school was a rough, wild school, but it made brave men.

When the nurse brought Jason to Chiron's cave, Chiron's wife took the child and cared for him as if he had been her own son, till he was old enough to profit by the centaur's teaching.

Meanwhile, Pelias reigned in Iolcus, and the true king, Æson, languished in prison. But the reign of Pelias, the usurper, was not altogether undisturbed. It was believed among the people that their rightful king would one day be restored to them; and there was a prophecy abroad which warned King Pelias to beware of a man who would one day come down from the mountains, wearing only one sandal.

When Jason was twenty years old, he was as well-developed and handsome a youth as any in Greece. His long waving hair fell down on his broad shoulders, and he had the sinewy walk of a young lion.

Being old enough now to try his strength, he bade good-bye, one day, to his good schoolmaster, Chiron, threw a leopard's skin over his shoulders, took a spear in each hand, and walked gaily down the road to Iolcus, for he meant to win back his kingdom from Pelias.

On his way down the mountain, he came to a stream which was badly swollen, and on the bank he saw an old woman who did not dare to cross. He kindly offered to carry her over, and his offer was accepted. He noticed that she looked very small and thin, and thought she would be very light to carry,

but when he had fairly entered the stream, he found
her very heavy. In his effort to fight against the
current, and at the same time to stand up under his
burden, he left one of his sandals sticking in the
mud at the bottom of the river. But he succeeded in
reaching the opposite shore, where he set the little
old woman down in safety. Then, what was his
astonishment to find that he had carried the great
goddess, Juno, across the stream. From this time
Juno was Jason's friend.

When he walked into the forum at Iolcus, the
people thought a god had come, and wondered
whether the stranger were not Apollo or Mars. But
King Pelias, remembering the prophecy, gave a quick
glance at Jason's feet, and saw only one sandal. With
much misgiving he asked the stranger's name.

Jason frankly told who he was, and how he had
been brought up in Chiron's cave. The news spread
quickly through the town, and Jason's kinsmen, the
sons of Æolus, heard it and welcomed him to their
houses.

After Jason had been in Iolcus for about five days,
he gathered his kinsmen together, and went before
the usurper, Pelias, and the people, to present his
claim to the throne. Since he and Pelias were kinsmen,
he did not think it right that there should be fighting
and bloodshed between them. So he consented to
give up to Pelias much of the land and many of the

flocks and herds which were his by right, but said that he must have the throne and sceptre.

Pelias showed no anger at this demand of Jason's, but he quickly devised a plan for sending the hero away again. He said that a few nights before Jason's arrival a very strange dream had come to him, in his sleep. In this dream a voice had commanded him to go to Colchis, and bring back the golden fleece of the ram which had carried Phrixus across the sea to Colchis.

The story of Phrixus was well known to Jason and to all the people of Iolcus. Many years before this, two little children, of the race of Æolus, Phrixus and Helle, who were persecuted by their step-mother, fled away from Iolcus by the help of a ram with a golden fleece. The ram had taken the two children on its back, and had swum away across the sea to the kingdom of Colchis. On the way, at a place where the water was very rough, Helle had fallen off and been drowned; but Phrixus had clung tightly to the ram's fleece, and arrived safe at Colchis. There the ram was sacrificed to Jupiter. Phrixus gave its beautiful golden fleece to the king of Colchis, who nailed it on a great oak tree, in the Garden of Mars. All these things had happened so very, very long before this, that the people of Iolcus had now almost forgotten that any such children as Phrixus and Helle had ever lived; but they remembered what their fathers had told them about the wonderful golden fleece of the ram, and many of them thought that the fleece should be brought back to Iolcus.

After telling his dream, King Pelias went on to say: "I should like nothing better than to obey the voice I heard in my dream; but I am getting to be an old man, far too old for such an enterprise. You, Jason, are young and strong. You had better go in my place. If you succeed in this, and thereby prove yourself able to rule over the people of Iolcus, you shall have your father's crown and throne."

The chiefs who were in attendance on Pelias all thought this fair. They said that a young man's courage should be proved; that if Jason were really fit for the throne, he would bring back the fleece. Jason's uncles and cousins said that if he attempted this task, he should not go alone, for they knew of some of the dangers he would have to encounter.

Then King Pelias gave orders to the heralds to go into the market-place with their trumpets and proclaim the expedition, and to call for volunteers who would accompany Jason in his quest of the Golden Fleece.

The call was answered by the bravest young men from all parts of Greece. Some were already celebrated heroes, and more became celebrated in after-years. Among them were Castor and Pollux, Hercules, Orpheus, the wonderful poet and musician, Meleager, two sons of Boreas, who had purple wings like their father, two sons of Mercury, King Admetus, some of Jason's cousins, and even the son of Pelias himself.

The Greek chiefs ordered a ship for the heroes, larger than any ship that had ever been built before. It was to be a galley of sixty oars. As the trees that were to furnish the timber for this great ship were still standing in their mountain forests, there was ample time for the heroes to finish any piece of work that they might have in hand, and to bid good-bye to their friends.

II

THE VOYAGE OF THE ARGONAUTS

When the Argo, as the new ship was called, was ready for the voyage, the heroes went on board, and took up the oars. Jason, standing in the stern, prayed to Jupiter, and when he had finished his prayer, threw mead into the sea from a golden goblet. Then Orpheus struck his lyre, and the heroes all began to row in time to his music. As the Argo passed slowly out of the harbour, a breeze from the south came up and filled the sails. The crowd of people who stood watching on the shore all took this for a good omen.

In those days any one who sailed far out into the open sea was likely to encounter all sorts of strange monsters and unknown terrors. The Argonauts, as these heroes were called, from the name of their ship, the Argo, had not sailed so very many miles before they saw a number of Harpies hovering over a rocky cape that jutted out into the sea. The Harpies were great birds like giant vultures, with faces like women.

As the Argonauts came nearer the cape, they could see that these horrible Harpies were tormenting a blind old man who sat among the trees in his garden. Next they could see that the man wore a crown on his head, and must therefore be a king, and that he was trying to eat his breakfast, which had been placed before him on a small table. Just as he had raised a morsel of food to his mouth, a Harpy would swoop down with a great rush of wings, snatch the food, and carry it away.

The sons of Boreas, feeling sorry for the poor old king, spread their purple wings, which were larger and stronger than those of the Harpies, rushed out from the Argo, drove the Harpies away, and chased them over the mountains.

The blind old king, whose name was Phineus, was very grateful to the sons of Boreas. He asked where the Argonauts were going. When he found that they were going to Colchis in quest of the Golden Fleece, he told them how to contrive a safe passage through the Symplegades, two huge rocks which the Argonauts would have to pass when they entered the Black Sea.

Many and many a good ship had been crushed by

the Symplegades; for when a ship or any moving object passed between them, these rocks had a trick of whirling around on their bases, and then crashing together with a force that would grind almost any substance into powder. To avoid such a calamity, King Phineus told the Argonauts to send a dove through the narrow passage between the rocks; and the moment that the rocks, after closing, began to swing open again, to row the Argo through with all possible speed, before they could close a second time.

The next day, the Argo reached the Symplegades, which rose up out of the sea like two strong towers. Jason, following the advice of King Phineus, took the swiftest of his doves, and sent it through between them. The huge rocks came together with a roar like thunder, then began to move slowly back to their places. Quickly the Argo shot through. But before her rudder was quite clear of the rocks, it was caught between them, as they crashed together again, and was crushed to atoms. The heroes all shuddered at their narrow escape, and rowed the ship away from those cruel rocks as quickly as they could.

When all danger was over, Jason thought with pity of the hard fate of the dove. Just then the gentle bird came fluttering down from the blue sky, and lit on his shoulder, cooing and turning and spreading out its tail, as happy as if it knew that it had saved the

Argo's crew. Its white wings had been too swift for the rocks.

After this the Symplegades never crushed any more ships; for they had come together with such great force that they could not separate themselves again, but became one rock.

The Argonauts sailed a long way farther, and saw many strange things. One day they passed the Island of Mars, where the Stymphalian birds built their nests, and here they found two sons of Phrixus who had been shipwrecked. They took these men into their ship, and gave them food and clothing. From them they found out that Æetes, the king of Colchis, was a cruel and wicked man whom they would have good reason to fear; and that the Golden Fleece was guarded by a most frightful dragon. Soon after this they reached Colchis. They came into the harbour at night, and anchored the Argo among trees and thick-growing bushes, where it would not be likely to be discovered.

III

THE WINNING OF THE GOLDEN FLEECE

The next day, after a consultation with the heroes, Jason went straight to King Æetes, and told him on what errand he had come.

"Oho! so you wish to take the Golden Fleece home

with you?" said Æetes. "Well, take it! You are quite welcome. But first, I am sure, you will not object to doing one or two little things to oblige me. Just yoke my bulls there to the plough, and plough a few acres in the Field of Mars. Then sow some dragon's teeth that I will give you. These dragon's teeth, by the way, are a few of the teeth of the dragon that was killed by Cadmus. They were a present to me from Mars."

The words of King Æetes were very polite, but in his tone there was a hidden sneer. Some of the Argonauts remembered having heard that it was this king's practice to sacrifice to the gods all strangers who landed on his shores, just as he would sacrifice cattle or sheep.

Medea, the king's daughter, stood by his side when Jason presented himself, and her dark eyes lighted up at the sight of the hero's beauty. Medea was the niece of Circe, the famous enchantress, and she had learned from her aunt the use of many medicinal and poisonous herbs. She knew certain charms and enchantments, too, and had secret rooms in her father's palace where a kettle full of a mysterious mixture was always boiling, and where a little owl sat and looked out of dark corners with its big yellow eyes.

No one knew what King Æetes meant to do with the Argonauts, who were now in his power. But at any rate, he entertained them hospitably for several days.

During this time Medea contrived to find Jason alone, and gave him a powerful ointment made in her kettle. She also gave him a little violet flower, which had been brought from the banks of the river Lethe.

The very day after Jason had received these gifts from Medea, King Æetes proposed to entertain his guests by games held in the Field of Mars. After a few races had been run, the king said that Jason should now plough an acre with the bulls, and then sow the dragon's teeth; and that if he succeeded in this, he might take the Golden Fleece from the tree where it hung, and carry it home to Iolcus.

Then Æetes brought out his bulls, without any assistance from his slaves; for they were fiery and untamed, and no other hand would dare to touch them. They were magnificent animals, and were certainly strong enough to put an end to any man's life, should they desire to do so. Their white horns were tipped with sharp steel points, and their hoofs, of solid brass, made a great clattering on the stone-paved road, as they were led from their stable. Although gentle enough with King Æetes, there was a look in their eyes that meant danger.

After he had hitched the bulls to the plough, the king ploughed a furrow, which was so long and straight and deep that the field seemed cut in two.

When it was finished, he took the yoke from the bulls' necks, and let them go free.

Now it was Jason's turn. The two bulls had begun grazing in the farther end of the field. As Jason approached them, they lifted their heads and snorted, sending a shower of gleaming sparks flying from their nostrils. Then they began to bellow furiously, and to paw up the earth with their brass hoofs. The grass all around them took fire.

The people of Colchis were astonished to see that Jason dared to go near such creatures, but they did not know how he was protected. The truth is, he was covered from head to foot with the oil or ointment made from a magic herb, which Medea had given him; and although the flying sparks might hit him, they could not set him on fire. So he walked coolly up to the enraged animals, and put the yoke on their necks.

The rage of the bulls cooled when they saw that Jason was not afraid, and they allowed him to hitch them to the plough. So he ploughed his acre according to the agreement, and made his furrows as straight and deep as that of Æetes. If, when driven by the hand of a stranger, the bulls did breathe out a few sparks now and then, that was no more than was to be expected—even though the whole acre was left smoking.

King Æetes looked on at the ploughing in speechless

wonder. This was something he had never seen before. He had supposed that if Jason were foolish enough to dare attempt such a task as this, the poor young man would be killed instantly.

But the dragon's teeth had not yet been sown. "*Now*, we will see what happens," this wicked king said to himself, as he brought them out.

Jason took the teeth without a moment's hesitation, and sowed them in the furrows, then covered them deep. He had heard the story of Cadmus and the dragon's teeth, and only half believed it. But the teeth sprouted and grew now, just as they had in the time of Cadmus. First, a few steel spear-heads pricked up through the ground; then the soil all over the ploughed acre began to heave, and before Jason knew what had happened, there stood rows of warriors, all armed, and looking very fierce. Seeing Jason, the warriors all raised their spears with a great cry, and would have attacked him, had not Jason hurled a great stone in among them. Then each warrior thought he had been attacked by his brothers. So they all began to fight among themselves, and continued fighting till every one was slain. When the last armed warrior of the dragon's brood had fallen, the Argonauts set up a loud cheer for their leader, and brought wreaths and crowned him, as they were accustomed to do when a hero won in the games.

King Æetes could not now deny to Jason the right

to take the Golden Fleece; but he secretly hoped
that Jason would not be able to conquer the dragon
that guarded it. Yesterday he would not have believed
it possible that any one could conquer that dragon;
but now it was with some misgiving that he showed
the way to the Grove of Mars, where the Golden
Fleece hung.

The Grove of Mars stood in a valley or garden,
called the Garden of Mars, which could be entered
only through a narrow ravine between two high
rocks. A rapid stream ran between the rocks, and
sometimes the Dragon of the Fleece lay in this stream
to guard the way. Sometimes, too, the dragon used
to coil itself around the oak where the fleece hung.
It was always somewhere in the valley, and was sure
to be wakeful and watching.

Before Jason could reach the Garden of Mars, the
day was spent, and the moon had risen and was
flooding everything with her silvery light. Jason was
glad to see that the night would not be a dark one.
When he reached the stream between the two high
rocks, he looked sharply for the dragon, but it was
not there. Then, with some difficulty, he climbed
along the narrow path at the side of the stream, and
went down into the valley.

This Garden of Mars was certainly not a beautiful
garden. Everything in it seemed to have been struck
by a blight. The earth produced no grass, but was

covered instead by bare, brown rocks whose edges looked sharp and dangerous. The trees seemed to have lost their power of bearing leaves, and bore only thorns, while their branches were twisted into the most fantastic shapes.

Jason soon saw the Golden Fleece. It was glorious; the one bright spot in the whole garden.

It hung on a low branch of the giant oak, and seemed to throw off flakes of light. And there, coiled around the huge trunk of the oak, was the dragon. It was spotted and blotched, and had a sharp-pointed, fierce-looking crest. It looked very ugly and dangerous.

As Jason came nearer to the oak, the dragon raised its crest and began to roar and bellow so loud that the sound could be heard in Colchis. But, safe in his hand, Jason had the little violet flower which Medea had plucked on the banks of Lethe. He held this flower out before him, at arm's length, and the moment the dragon smelt its strange odour, it lowered the crest on its drooping head, closed its fierce eyes, and fell into a deep sleep.

Then Jason took down the beautiful Golden Fleece from the oak, and went to tell his Argonauts that he had conquered the dragon, as well as the fire-breathing bulls, and had obtained possession of the coveted fleece. They all agreed that they had better take the Argo and sail for home while it was still night.

When the heroes were getting the Argo under way, Medea stole away from the palace and joined them.

By the time the sun rose, the next morning, they were well out to sea. Word was brought to King Æetes that the Argonauts had taken the Golden Fleece and gone, and that Medea had gone with them. The king went down to the shore with a great company of armed men, and sent some of his war galleys after the Argo; but the Argo, leaving the Colchian ships far behind, soon passed swiftly out of sight, and the angry king was left standing on the Colchian shore.

The heroes reached Iolcus in safety, and there Jason reigned long and happily in the place of King Pelias, the usurper.

19

Hylas

WHEN Jason sailed away on the famous quest of the Golden Fleece, Hercules was one of the heroes who accompanied him. At that time, Hercules took with him, on the Argo, a beautiful boy named Hylas, who served him as page. Hercules was very fond of this boy. He dressed him in green with gold lace, and kept him at his side all day long, teaching him to use the bow and arrow, to throw the discus, and to do many other things that he himself had learned from his father or from the herdsmen of Mount Cithæron.

After the Argonauts had sailed for three days, with a fresh south wind filling their sails, they came to a small sea called the Propontis, and there, the wind failing, they drew the Argo up on the beach, and went ashore. At the spot where they landed, they found salt meadows, all abloom with beautiful flowers of every colour. They gathered the tall reeds and the flowering flags, flowers and all, with other marsh plants, and made comfortable beds for themselves under the cool shade of the trees, in order to get a few hours' sleep; for they knew that during

the heat of the day they could not make much head-
way in rowing.

Toward night they all set about getting supper,
and Hylas, for his part, took a pitcher and went to
draw water for Hercules. He found, in a low, marshy
place, a spring of fresh water, so large that it was like
a pond. Rushes and delicate wild grasses grew all
around it; ferns leaned over the edge of the water;
and a kind of climbing milkweed, like a wax-plant,
made the air sweet with its white blossoms. It was a
beautiful spring, and the water-nymphs had taken it
for their own. They lived down at the bottom of this
spring, and used to come up and dance around among
the flowers, by moonlight.

Hylas knew nothing of the nymphs, but when he
stood over the water, and began to fill the pitcher,
he heard a chorus of silvery voices saying, "Come
down! Come down!" The nymphs had seen him, and
they admired his beautiful face and the gold lace he
wore.

While he was looking into the spring, and wondering what the voices were, and what they could
mean, two slender white hands suddenly reached up
from the black water and pulled him down.

When it began to grow dark, and Hylas did not
come back, Hercules, fearing that some mishap had
befallen the boy, took his club in one hand and his
bow in the other, and went to look for him. As he

walked inland, in the direction that Hylas had taken, he called as loud as he could,—and that was very loud indeed,—"Hylas! Hylas!" The call came echoing back from the hills, "Hylas! Hylas!" and that was all the answer that Hercules got, till he passed close to the nymphs' spring. Then he thought he heard Hylas's own voice answering faintly; but as it seemed to come from so very, very far away, he never dreamed that his little page could be down under the black water, and went on, tearing his way through the briers to no purpose.

At midnight a breeze sprang up. Then the Argonauts left their beds of rushes, hoisted the sails of the ship, and made ready to go—but where was Hercules? The heroes waited for him a long time; then, saying that he was a runaway and did not mean to go with them to Colchis, they took up the anchor and went on without him.

Poor Hercules roamed the hills and searched through all the marshes for three days. More than once he heard that faint voice answering his call; but he never could tell where it came from, and so made up his mind that it was his own imagination. At last he gave up the search, and went on to Colchis on foot.

Hylas, not knowing that Hercules had gone, kept on calling to his friend, "Hercules, Hercules, here I am!" Several peasants who passed that way heard his voice, but could not tell where it came from, any more than Hercules could. Still the voice called, all night long, for many nights, "Hercules, Hercules!"

Some time after, one of these peasants saw a little creature, not more than an inch or two long, sitting on a reed. It was clothed in green with gold lace, just as the lost page had been. Tiny as it was, it had a voice out of all proportion to its size. While the peasant stood looking at it, it puffed out its throat and called loudly, but all it said was, "Hr-r-reep! Hreep! Hreep!"

20

Procne and Philomela

KING PANDION had two beautiful daughters, called Procne and Philomela. It came about that the eldest, Procne, was married to King Tereus, who was the son of Mars, the cruel god of war. The wedding festivities lasted for two weeks, or more, with singing and dancing, and much other merrymaking; but Hymen, the little marriage-god, was not present among the guests with his torch, neither were the Graces. This was a bad omen, as it meant ill-fortune for the bride; but it was a much worse one when a little owl came in, flew to the rafters overhead, and began to hoot dismally.

After Procne had been married a few years, she felt so lonely in the great palace in Thrace, that she begged King Tereus either to let her go home or to send for her sister, Philomela.

King Tereus said that her sister should come to her. He ordered a ship launched, and went himself to bring Philomela.

King Pandion did not like to part from his younger daughter, who was the only child he had left; but

Philomela wished so much to see her sister that she
put her arms around her father's neck, and coaxed
him to let her go, until at last he gave a reluctant
consent.

Now, alas for Philomela, King Tereus was a very
cruel, wicked man. When he saw how beautiful this
younger sister was, he wished that he had married
her instead of Procne. As soon as the ship reached
Thrace, he sent Procne away into a great forest,
where he had her shut up in a lonely tower. Then,
sighing and groaning, he told Philomela that her
sister was dead. Philomela was heart-broken, and
mourned a long time; but nevertheless she was finally
persuaded to become the queen of King Tereus, in
Procne's place.

The king's wicked plan had succeeded thus far,
but he feared that Procne might tell how cruelly she
had been treated. This fear made him more cruel
still, for he had her tongue cut out, thus making the
poor queen dumb.

Now he thought all was safe, but he did not know
how skilful Procne was at her weaving and her
embroidery. She had never learned to write—even
queens could not write in those days; but she could
weave most wonderful pictures, and could embroider
letters, and put them together to form a few simple
words. She needed nothing more to make her story
known. For almost a year she worked busily at her

loom and with her needle. Then one day she sent one of her maids to Philomela at the palace, with the gift of a piece of tapestry.

When Philomela unrolled the tapestry and spread it out before her, she was horrified at what she saw, for she easily understood all that Procne had meant to tell her by the woven pictures.

She immediately sent for her sister, by night. The two then planned to fly from the country of King Tereus, taking Procne's little son, Itys, with them. As they stole out of the palace, the great doors creaked on their rusty hinges, and awoke the king. He came rushing out, with a drawn sword, and started in pursuit of the fugitives.

Philomela and Procne ran as fast as they could, dragging Itys between them; but the wicked King Tereus was getting nearer and nearer.

All at once the sisters felt themselves borne up on the air, and carried along as if they had wings. The gods, in pity, had changed them into birds. Procne became a swallow; Philomela, a nightingale. The child, Itys, being in no danger from his father's anger, was not changed into a bird, and was therefore left behind.

Procne, now a swift-winged swallow, went back to the palace many a day, lingered under the eaves, and even flew in at the open doors, trying to coax her child to come away with her. But Itys saw only a pretty, bright-eyed bird, and could not understand its excited chatter.

Philomela, even as a bird, remained broken-hearted. She hid away from other birds, and remained silent while they were singing. At night, however, when all was dark and still, she used to sing under the windows of the peasants, telling the story of her dumb sister's wrongs, and her own sorrow.

21

Bellerophon

WHEN the summer suns had scorched the plains and
dried the rivers of Greece till hardly any green thing
was left, there were meadows, high on the snowy
sides of Mount Helicon, that were bright with soft
young grasses, and dotted with flowers of every
colour.

In these meadows were the most glorious fountains.
At certain times they sent their waters spouting far
up into the blue sky, whence they came tumbling
down again, to rise once more in a fine spray, in
which could be seen a thousand rainbows.

The most beautiful fountain of all, and the one
where the water was the sweetest and the coolest,
was called the Fountain of Hippocrene. The waters
of this fountain had a wonderful magic. There had
been a time when no such fountain was to be seen
on Mount Helicon. One bright moonlight night
Pegasus, the winged horse, alighted in these meadows.
He uttered a silvery neigh, and then struck the ground
a sharp blow with his hoof. Immediately this Fountain
of Hippocrene gushed forth. Pegasus drank of its

sweet waters, and then flew away, far above the clouds. But he sometimes came back to drink of those waters again. There was no place on earth where a plain mortal would be more likely to see him.

The Muses, too, haunted these beautiful meadows of Helicon. They were nine sisters, with hair so black that it seemed violet in the moonlight. On nights when a full moon was in the sky, they used to come and dance around the Fountain of Hippocrene. Some people believed that Pegasus belonged to them.

Shepherds who fed their sheep at the foot of Mount Helicon, and watched all night long, lest some prowling wolf should attack the flock, sometimes caught a glimpse of Pegasus or the Muses; but very few people in the towns below even believed that either the winged horse or the nine sisters really existed at all.

Now it happened one day that a certain young hero, named Bellerophon, came to Mount Helicon to look for Pegasus. He had been sent by a king to slay the Chimæra, a kind of monstrous dragon with three heads, that was laying waste the country in a certain part of Asia. He thought that, with the help of the winged horse, he might win an easy victory over any earth-born monster.

So, night after night, Bellerophon came to the Fountain of Hippocrene and watched for Pegasus. For a long time he could not see so much as a feather of the horse's glorious wings; although, once or twice, when the moon was shining more brightly than usual, he did think that a shadow passed lightly over the grass, but when he looked up, there was nothing to be seen. Another time he heard a sudden rush of wings, and caught a glimpse of something white among the trees.

At last, it chanced one night that he found a lost child on the lower slopes of Mount Helicon, and knowing that it was in great danger of being devoured by wild beasts, he took it to one of the shepherds who were watching their sheep near by. Then he went on to the spring, where he arrived much later than usual.

That night he saw Pegasus careering gaily about the meadows. The horse's silvery wings were held high over his back, and his dainty pink hoofs scarcely touched the ground. His whinnying was like the tremulous music of a flute; but when he saw Bellerophon, he spread his great white wings, and soared away up into the depths of the sky.

Catch Pegasus! Bellerophon saw that it was of no use to try, and gave it up. Then he lay down and slept on the soft grass of the meadow.

But people who slept near the Fountain of Hippocrene were apt to dream. While Bellerophon slept, he dreamed that Minerva stood at his side with a golden bridle in her hand. In the dream she gave him the bridle, and then Pegasus came up to him, and bent his beautiful head to have it put on.

He woke in the morning with the first sunbeams shining in his face, and found the golden bridle of his dream in his hands. The head-piece was set with jewels, and the whole bridle was so gorgeous that it seemed fit, even for so wonderful a horse as Pegasus.

Bellerophon did not go down to the town that day, but stayed on Mount Helicon, and lived on berries and sweet acorns. When night came, he again waited by the fountain for Pegasus.

With a light heart, he went to his usual place, where he was screened by the bushes. He had hardly seated himself before he saw a faint white speck in the sky, which grew larger and larger, and soon took the shape of a winged horse.

As the beautiful creature descended lower, he began to fly in great circles, as you have seen a hawk fly. But his shining white wings were more like the wings of an albatross than like those of any other bird we know. He came lower, and lower, till his feet touched the meadow; and then he cantered up to Bellerophon, and held down his head for the jewelled bridle, just as he had done in Bellerophon's dream. A moment more, and the bridle was over his head.

A more gentle horse than Pegasus never lived, nor one fonder of his rider. He seemed willing to take the owner of the bridle for his master, and was obedient to the slightest touch of the rein. It was wonderful when he tried his wings. Up above the clouds he soared, with Bellerophon on his back. Who need fear the Chimæra now?

This Chimæra was a frightful monster with three heads—the head of a lion, the head of a goat, and the head of a snake. Its body was something like the shaggy body of a goat in the middle, but ended in a dragon's tail. When the creature was roused, it could belch out fire and smoke from its three cavernous throats. Nearly the whole of the mountainous country it inhabited was a waste of ashes. The few people who had not lost their lives, nor left their homes and their flocks, but still inhabited that region, lived in constant terror of this creature. So if one brave enough and strong enough could be found, there was need of a hero to slay the Chimæra.

When Bellerophon felt that he had perfect control of Pegasus, he guided him straight toward the mountains of the Chimæra. Pegasus, with all his wonderful power of flight, sped through the air like an arrow, and in a very short time was hovering over the cruel monster, which lay sprawling in the midst of the waste it had caused.

Obedient to Bellerophon's wish, Pegasus swooped straight down to within striking distance of the Chimæra. Then, a flash from Bellerophon's lance, and the goat's head hung limp. What a roar followed from the lion's head! All the air became filled with the sickening odour, and it began to grow dark with smoke. But Bellerophon and Pegasus were safe, high above the earth.

They waited till the monster was quiet again, then made another quick dash, and off went the lion's head. There was no roaring this time, and not so much fire and smoke, although the angry writhing of the creature was terrible to see. But the Chimæra could not follow Pegasus into the pure upper air.

Once more horse and rider dashed down, and the snake's head was severed from the Chimæra's body. Then the terrible fires burned themselves out, and that was the end of the Chimæra.

The people of that country soon learned that the Chimæra was dead, and came back to their homes. Not long after, the hills, that had been so gray and desolate, were covered with vineyards and growing crops.

After this, Bellerophon, with the help of Pegasus, performed other wonderful feats, and became very famous. He married a king's daughter, and received half of her father's kingdom.

At last he felt as if, mounted on Pegasus, he was as strong as the gods themselves, and might ascend to Olympus. One day he was foolish enough to make the attempt. Then Jupiter caused Pegasus to throw him. Blinded by the near sight of Olympus, and lamed by the fall, he wandered about, for many years, an unhappy, helpless old man.

The time came when the gods took Pegasus up to Mount Olympus, and let us hope that Bellerophon, too, reached Olympus at last.

22

Tithonus

EVERY day, when Helios drove his wonderful horses and his fiery chariot across the sky, it was Aurora who opened the gates of pearl and drew back the dark curtains of the night; for Aurora was the goddess of the dawn. She was so beautiful that the whole sky flushed pink with pleasure when she appeared in the east.

On the earth lived a mortal called Tithonus, who loved Aurora so well that he never failed to leave his bed while it was still dark, to watch for her coming. Aurora loved Tithonus in return, and one day she flew to the king of the gods, and begged of him that Tithonus might be given a draught of nectar, and so become immortal.

Jupiter granted this request, and Aurora took Tithonus up to Mount Olympus to live in her golden house.

The goddess had forgotten to ask that Tithonus might never grow old. Therefore, the time came when gray hairs could be seen among his golden curls. Aurora was kind to him in spite of this, and continued to give him beautiful garments, and to feed him on ambrosia. Still, Tithonus grew older and older, and in time, after several hundred years, he was so very old that he could not move at all. Little was left of him but his voice, and even that had grown high and thin. Then he withered away so much that he had to be shut up in a room, for safe-keeping. Aurora felt so sorry to see him withering away in this manner that she changed him into a little insect, and sent him down to the earth again, where men called him the grasshopper.

Very glad to be free and active once more, Tithonus hopped about in the fields all day, chirping cheerfully to Aurora.

23

Comatas and the Honey-bees

LONG, long after the days of Bellerophon, a certain goatherd, called Comatas, used to feed his goats on the lower slopes of Mount Helicon.

While watching the goats, he would lie under the pine trees, and play on his shepherd's pipe. Sometimes, when the nights were warm, instead of driving his goats home to the fold, he used to stay on the mountain with them, during the night as well as the day. He had once seen the Muses dancing round the Fountain of Hippocrene, in the moonlight.

Not far from the fountain was a small altar which belonged to the Muses. Comatas thought he would like to bring some gift to it; but he was a slave, and had not a thing in the world which he could call his own. As he spent his life in the care of the goats, he felt that they must belong to him, in part. So, one day, he took a kid from the flock, and sacrificed it on the altar.

That night the master counted the goats, and found one missing. In a violent passion, he took Comatas and put him into a great chest which stood in his palace hall. Then he shut down the lid and locked the chest, leaving the poor goatherd to die of starvation.

But the Muses had not forgotten their worshipper. They missed the sound of his piping, on the grassy slopes of Mount Helicon. Certain great purple moths used to flutter around with them in their moonlight dances. They sent one of these to find out what had become of the goatherd.

The moth flew straight to the huts of the slaves, but it did not find Comatas there. Then it flew in at one of the palace windows. The master of Comatas was sitting at a long table, with his friends, drinking wine. The purple moth took a sip from one of the goblets, then it fluttered airily round one of the tall bronze lamps. Next it crawled over the hangings, where there was a whole field of flowers, done in embroidery. Soon tiring of embroidered flowers, which had no sweetness, it descended to the floor, where it was attracted by the odour of the cedar-chest. Crawling up over the side of the chest, it peeped in at the keyhole, and found Comatas. Then it flew quickly away to Mount Helicon, to tell the Muses.

The next day a honey-bee flew in at the palace gate. It met the master of Comatas, and gave him a fine sting on the nose. Not long after, the housemaids or the guards, if they had been looking, might have seen another bee crawling up the carved side of the cedar-chest, and going in at the keyhole, which was a door quite large enough for a honey-bee.

Soon other bees came, with their honey-bags full. They went in at the same tiny door, and came out again with their honey-bags empty.

One day, after Comatas had been shut up in the chest a year, his hard-hearted master caused the chest to be opened, expecting, of course, to find nothing but a handful of bones. There sat Comatas alive and well! This was wonderful, indeed.

Comatas told how he had been fed by the bees. His master, knowing that all honey-bees were the special servants of the Muses, believed that the Muses themselves had taken Comatas under their protection, and thereafter treated him with the greatest respect and the utmost kindness.

24

Adonis

ADONIS was young, gentle, and very beautiful. All things loved him. Flowers sprang up under his feet, and bees and butterflies fluttered around him. When he went out hunting in the forest with his hounds, Venus, the goddess of beauty, used to follow him at a distance, keeping within the shadows. She trembled lest some accident should befall him, for she knew that the forest was full of wolves, panthers, and other beasts even more dangerous.

Mars, the cruel war-god, hated all gentle and beautiful things, and he hated Adonis worst of all. One day he sent an ugly wild boar, with his great sharp tusks, to attack the boy.

A few hours later Venus found Adonis, wounded and dying, with the bright blood falling in drops from his side. She bent over him, her tears falling with the drops of blood. As Venus's tears touched the ground, they were changed to wind-flowers, while every drop of blood that fell from the wound of Adonis became a red rose.

When bright Adonis went down to the dark

underworld, all things on earth mourned for him. The flowers faded in the fields, the trees cast down their leaves, the dolphins wept near the shore, and the nightingales sang the saddest songs they knew. The Muses cried, "Woe, woe for Adonis! He hath perished, the lovely Adonis!" And Echo, from the dark forests where the youth had so often hunted, answered, "He hath perished, the lovely Adonis!"

At last Jupiter said that Adonis should return, and that he should spend at least one-half of his time in the upper world and the other half in the underworld. So the Hours brought him back.

Then the flowers sprang up again, the trees put forth new leaves, and all became light-hearted and happy once more.

25

King Midas

I

KING MIDAS AND THE GOLDEN TOUCH

It happened one day that Silenus, who was the oldest of the satyrs and was now very feeble, became lost in the vineyards of King Midas. The peasants found him wandering helplessly about, scarcely able to walk, and brought him to the king.

Long ago, when the mother of Bacchus had died, and when Mercury had brought the infant Bacchus to this mountain and put him in the care of the nymphs, Silenus had acted as nurse and teacher to the little wine-god. Now that Silenus had grown old, Bacchus in turn took care of him. So King Midas sent the peasants to carry the satyr safely to Bacchus.

In return for this kindness, Bacchus promised to grant whatever King Midas might ask. King Midas knew well enough what he most desired. In those days, kings had treasuries in their palaces, that is, safe places where they could lay away valuable things. The treasury of King Midas contained a vast collection of rich jewels, vessels of silver and gold, chests of gold coins, and other things that he considered precious.

When Midas was a very little child, he used to watch the ants running back and forth over the sand near his father's palace. It seemed to him that the ant-hill was like another palace, and that the ants were working very hard carrying in treasure; for they came running to the ant-hill from all directions, carrying little white bundles. Midas made up his mind, then, that when he grew up, he would work very hard and gather treasure together.

Now that he was a man, and the king, nothing gave him more pleasure than to add to the collection in his treasury. He was continually devising ways of exchanging or selling various things, or contriving some new tax for the people to pay, and turning all into gold or silver. In fact, he had gathered treasure together so industriously, and for so many years, that he had begun to think that the bright yellow gold in his chests was the most beautiful and the most precious thing in the world.

So when Bacchus offered him anything that he might ask for, King Midas's first thought was of his treasury, and he asked that whatever he touched might be turned into gold. His wish was granted.

King Midas was hardly able to believe in his good fortune. He thought himself the luckiest of men.

At the time his wish was granted he happened to stand under an oak tree, and the first thing he did was to raise his hand and touch one of its branches. Immediately the branch became the richest gold, with all the little acorns as perfect as ever. He laughed triumphantly at that, and then he touched a small stone, which lay on the ground. This became a solid gold nugget. Then he picked an apple from a tree, and held a beautiful, bright, gold apple in his hand. Oh, there was no doubt about it. King Midas really had the Golden Touch! He thought it too good to be true. After this he touched the lilies that bordered the walk. They turned from pure white to bright yellow, but bent their heads lower than ever, as if they were ashamed of the change that the touch of King Midas had wrought in them.

Before turning any more things into gold, the king sat down at the little table which his slaves had brought out into the court. The parched corn was fresh and crisp, and the grapes juicy and sweet. But when he tasted a grape from one of the luscious clusters, it became a hard ball of gold in his mouth. This was very unpleasant. He laid the gold ball on the table and tried the parched wheat, but only to have his mouth filled with hard yellow metal. Feeling as if he were choking, he took a sip of water, and at the touch of his lips even this became liquid gold.

Then all his bright treasures began to look ugly to

him, and his heart grew as heavy as if that, too, were turning to gold.

That night King Midas lay down under a gorgeous golden counterpane, with his head upon a pillow of solid gold; but he could not rest, sleep would not come to him. As he lay there, he began to fear that his queen, his little children, and all his kind friends, might be changed to hard, golden statues.

This would be more deplorable than anything else that had resulted from his foolish wish. Poor Midas saw now that riches were not the most desirable of all things. He was cured forever of his love of gold. The instant it was daylight he rushed to Bacchus, and implored the god to take back his fatal gift.

"Ah," said Bacchus, smiling, "so you have gold enough, at last. Very well. If you are sure that you do not wish to change anything more into that metal, go and bathe in the spring where the river Pactolus rises. The pure water of that spring will wash away the Golden Touch."

King Midas gladly obeyed, and became as free from the Golden Touch as when he was a boy watching the ants. But the strange magic was imparted to the waters of the spring, and to this day the river Pactolus has golden sands.

II

WHY KING MIDAS HAD ASSES' EARS

AFTER his strange experience with the Golden Touch, King Midas did not care for the things in his treasure chests any more, but left them to the dust and the spiders, and went out into the fields, and followed Pan.

Pan was the god of the flocks, the friend of shepherds and country folk. He lived in a cave, which was in a mountain not far from the palace of Midas. He was sometimes seen, playing on his pipe, or dancing with the forest nymphs. He had horns and legs like a goat, and furry, pointed ears.

Pan was a sunny, careless, happy-go-lucky kind of god, and when he sat playing on his pipe—which he himself had made—the music came bubbling forth in such a jolly way that it set the nymphs to dancing, and the birds to singing.

When King Midas heard Pan's pipe, he used to forget that he was a king, or that he had any cares whatever. He was content to feel the warmth of the sun, and breathe the sweet air of the mountain.

One day Pan boasted to the nymphs, in a joking way, that the music of his pipe was better than that of Apollo's lyre. The nymphs laughed, and said that he and Apollo ought to play together, with Tmolus, the god of the mountain, for the judge. Pan said that he was ready to try his skill against Apollo's. Tmolus consented to be the judge. So a day was appointed for the contest.

Apollo came with his lyre. He had a laurel crown on his head, and wore a rich purple robe which swept the ground. His lyre, which was a beautiful instrument, was made of gold, and was inlaid with ivory and precious stones. This made Pan's pipe, which consisted of seven pieces of a hollow reed lightly joined together, look very simple and rustic.

Both Apollo and Pan began to play. Tmolus turned toward Apollo, to listen, and all his trees turned with him. Before they had played long, the mountain-god stopped Pan, saying, "You must know that your simple pipe cannot compare with Apollo's wonderful lyre."

Pan took this in good part; he knew that the contest had been only a joke. While the nymphs and the shepherds made light of the decision against their friend, Midas, who could not appreciate the lyre, but who was just suited by the music of the pipe, jumped up and cried out, "This is unjust! Pan's music is better than that of Apollo!"

At this, all but Apollo laughed. He was angry. He looked severely at the ears of Midas, which must have heard so crudely. All at once King Midas felt his ears growing long and furry. He clapped his hands over them, and rushed to a spring near by, where he could see himself. His ears had been changed into those of an ass.

So Midas was punished by the gods a second time for his foolishness. He was very much ashamed of those long, furry ears, and always after that wore a great, purple turban to hide them.

One day, when the court-barber was cutting Midas's hair, he discovered the king's secret, and was so much astonished that he dropped his shears on the floor with a great clatter. He knew he might lose his head if he should tell what he had seen. So he said not a word to any mortal soul; but one day, to relieve his mind, he went to a lonely place, dug a hole in the ground, and whispered what he had seen to the earth. Then he put the soil back, and so buried the secret.

But after a secret has once been told, it is not so easy to hide it. After about a year, some reeds grew up in that place. When the south wind blew, they whispered together all day, and told one another that, under his turban, King Midas had asses' ears. And so the secret was spread abroad.

26

The King and the Oak

THERE was once a beautiful grove, in Thessaly, which was sacred to Ceres. The trees in it had been growing there for nobody knows how many hundreds of years. They were very, very large, and their great branches grew so close together that scarcely a ray of sunshine could penetrate to the ground underneath.

It was cool in this grove, even on the hottest summer day. Little fawns and their mothers lay on the pine needles in the shade, feeling safer there than anywhere else. Birds sang from the tops of the tallest trees, and many a nest was hidden under their leaves.

The temple of the goddess stood in an open glade, in which were sparkling fountains, whose waters kept everything fresh and green. Here grew the grandest tree of all, a gigantic oak, so tall that its top seemed to reach almost to heaven. Its lower branches were thickly hung with wreaths, and votive tablets, on which were written the thanks of people who had received the help of Ceres.

Every tree in this grove was inhabited by a hamadryad, or wood-nymph, whose life was bound up in that of the tree in which she lived. If the trees died, the hamadryads would die too. Such groves were never cut. At noon, all these nymphs used to dance around the great oak, and sometimes Pan, with his little horns and goats' feet, came and danced with them.

Close by, a king of that country was building a new palace. When the walls were finished, he wanted timbers for the roof. One day he came into the grove of Ceres, bringing with him twenty woodmen, each of whom carried an axe or a saw.

The king told the woodmen to begin at once and cut down every tree in the grove, but the men, knowing that the grove was sacred to Ceres, and that the trees in it had been allowed to grow undisturbed for more than a thousand years, hesitated about carrying out such an order.

Then the king, in a fine temper, caught up an axe, and with a ringing stroke sent its blade into the trunk of the beautiful oak. A shriek followed the stroke of the axe. It was the voice of the hamadryad; but the king said that it was only the singing of the axe, and he would not stop.

Just then the old priestess came out from the temple, and told the king very gently that it would not be wise to anger Ceres; and she reminded him that the goddess had power over everything that grows out of the earth.

At this the king's strokes only flew the faster, and he spoke in a very insolent manner to the kind old priestess. "Stand off," said he, "the axe may hit you. The next time you see your trees they will be in my palace roof."

Without another word, the priestess walked quietly away; but a strange expression came into her face, which suddenly bore a close resemblance to that of Ceres herself.

Soon, the great oak fell, with a crash. There was a moan from the dying hamadryad, and an answering wail from the other nymphs of the grove. The woodmen were frightened, and would gladly have spared the other trees; but the king insisted that every one should be cut.

The king's palace was soon completed, and it was a most magnificent structure. All went so well that the king began to think Ceres had forgotten his destruction of her sacred grove, or had not the power to punish him for it.

But the punishment came soon enough. At the command of Ceres, Famine now came to Thessaly. Famine, a servant of Ceres, was a frightful old creature, who, wherever she went, pulled up every green and growing thing, and then sowed hunger broadcast. On the approach of Famine, the beautiful fountains in the grove of Ceres, which had fed nearly all the rivers in the kingdom, began to dry up, and the rivers they had fed became nothing more than little brooks. The rain ceased to fall, and all crops failed. The peasants became discouraged, and, one by one, they took their goods and their flocks and herds, and went away to other lands.

One night, in spite of guarded gates and bolted doors, Famine walked into the king's own palace, and then the king himself learned what it was to be hungry. He laid the blame on his servants, and treated them so badly that they left him, one after another. At last there was left in the whole kingdom only the king and his one daughter, Metra, who was faithful to her father through all his troubles.

Ceres still withheld the rain, and scarcely any living thing could grow. Where the fields had been green, and where flocks of sheep and great herds of cattle had once fed, there was now only bare sand. Travellers still passed along the highway in front of the king's palace, on their way to and from a rich city on the coast. The only way that the king and Metra could obtain food now was to sit by the highway and beg of these strangers.

Finally, tortured by hunger, the king one day sold his daughter as a slave to a passing merchant. By this means he obtained sufficient food to supply his wants for some time; but even this store of food, so dearly bought, could not last, and there came a time when the poor king was worse off than ever. His kingdom had become a desert; his last friend was gone. How gladly he would have given his magnificent palace and the empty honour of being king of a forsaken country, if he could have seen the great oak growing again, and his kingdom fertile and flourishing as it had once been. But it was now too late. Even Ceres could not make the trees of her sacred grove grow again, nor bring back the wood-nymphs who had inhabited them.

27

Juno and Halcyone

JUNO, sitting on her golden throne on Mount Olympus, could look down and see all that happened on the earth. She watched over the fortunes of good women among mortals, and was the special protectress of brides. Her two special birds—the peacock and the cuckoo—might often be seen near her. On the steps of her throne slept her messenger, Iris, always half-awake, and ready to dart down like a bird, to the earth, to the underworld, or to any other place where Juno might send her.

Iris was the granddaughter of Old Ocean. Her sisters were the Dark Clouds; her bridge was the rainbow, which joined heaven to earth. She had golden wings, and her draperies were as many-coloured as her bridge, which was made of the most beautiful flower-tints ever seen.

One of Juno's most faithful worshippers was Halcyone, the wife of King Ceyx of Thessaly. It happened that King Ceyx was obliged to take a distant journey, far away over the seas. One night during his absence a very heavy storm came up, and the winds blew a gale.

Halcyone, being the daughter of the wind-god, Æolus, knew well what her brothers, the Winds, could do, and passed the night in great terror. The next day she walked back and forth all day on the shore, longing for tidings of her husband's ship, yet fearing to know what might have happened. She was almost beside herself, and did not know what to do. At last, toward night, she carried wreaths to Juno's temple, and implored help from the goddess.

Juno knew all that had happened during the storm —how the king's ship had been broken to pieces upon the rocks, and how poor King Ceyx was already floating with the seaweed.

But the gods could do wonderful things. At a word from Juno, Iris set her beautiful rainbow bridge in the sky, while her sisters, the Dark Clouds, gathered together behind it. She came swiftly down the bridge to the earth, then flew toward the cave of Somnus, the god of sleep and dreams. She flew low over great fields of scarlet poppies—the poppies that bring sleep—and heard the trickling water of the river Lethe, which had its source within the cave of Somnus. Soon she reached the dark, cool, silent cave, and there lay Somnus, sleeping very soundly, on a great bed heaped high with black feathers. Around the god were dreams of every kind—good dreams and bad ones, beautiful and ugly, true and false. As Iris entered, her coming lighted up the darkness, and the wonderful colours of her garments were reflected to the farthest recess of the cave. She roused Somnus and delivered Juno's message.

That night Somnus sent a dream to Halcyone,—a dream of a wreck at a place some distance down the coast. Early the next morning, Halcyone ran to the place of which she had dreamed. She saw floating beams, and something bright among them—something which shone like the king's crown. Having a sudden longing to go to this spot, she started forward, and immediately felt herself raised on wings and carried out over the tossing waves, for Juno had changed her into a bird with plumage of Iris's own colours. With a loud cry, Halcyone flew to her Ceyx. Just as she lit on the floating beams, the bright crown became a crest of feathers, and the dead king a living bird with plumage like Halcyone's own.

So, after all, Ceyx and Halcyone were not separated. The air was as fresh and the sunshine as bright as ever. They could still be happy as king-fishers. After this, every year, the two birds built a nest which floated on the sea. During the fourteen days that Halcyone sat brooding, there was never a breath of wind stirring, but the sea was as smooth as glass, for Æolus watched over the waters. From that time, days of fine weather and calm seas, in midwinter, have been called "halcyon days."

28

Hercules

I

HERCULES IN HIS CRADLE

AMONG all the heroes about whom the old Greek harpers used to sing, was one who was better loved by the Greek people than any of the rest. This was Hercules. He was loved by the Greeks better than any of their other heroes, because he was stronger and braver than any of the others.

Hercules performed his first brave deed when he was a mere baby, less than a year old. It happened in this way. One day Alcmene, the mother of Hercules, after bathing her twin babies, Hercules and Iphicles, fed them and put them into the hollow bronze shield which served for their cradle, and then sang them a lullaby, and rocked them to sleep. That night, when all the house was still, two huge snakes, whose bite was deadly, crawled in under the great doors, and came slowly across the floor to the place where the two babies were sleeping. The snakes lifted their heads above the shield, and with their wicked little eyes looked down at the children, but waited for some movement from them before striking. Just then both babies woke. Hercules sat up in the shield, and quick as a flash, caught both snakes by the neck, and began to squeeze their throats with all his might. Iphicles screamed, and then began to cry, while the snakes writhed and twisted and beat the floor with their tails.

Alcmene, hearing the noise, woke the children's father, Amphitryon. He hastily took his sword from the peg at the head of his bed, and calling on his slaves to bring torches, entered the room where the children were, not knowing what enemy he might see.

There sat little Hercules, holding two great snakes by their necks, and crowing with pleasure, as if he had found a new plaything. When his father came to the side of the shield, Hercules laid the two snakes at his feet, quite dead. You may believe Amphitryon was astonished.

The next morning Alcmene asked a wise old man, called Tiresias, what it meant that a baby, only ten months old, had been able to kill two great snakes. Tiresias answered that Hercules, when he grew up, should be stronger than any wild beast, or than any other man who had ever lived, and that he should perform twelve wonderful labours, and afterward should live on Mount Olympus, with the gods.

II

THE YOUTH OF HERCULES

As Hercules grew up, he was carefully trained in all the things that Greek boys were accustomed to learn. He was taught his letters, how to play on the lyre, and how to shoot with the bow and arrow. He was taught by his father how to drive, standing in his chariot, as the Greeks drove in their races. He also learned how to box, to wrestle, to throw the discus, and to fight with the lance and shield. During the day he was always at his father's side, and at night his bed, which was covered with a lion's skin, stood near that of his father.

When he was almost grown, he went to live, for a time, among the herdsmen on the mountains. He lay down one day in a lonely spot in one of the mountain valleys, to sleep through the noonday heat. In his sleep he had a strange dream. It seemed to him in his dream that the path he was following suddenly divided into two well-marked roads, and he could not tell which he ought to take. One looked very smooth and easy to follow, and seemed to lead, a little farther down the mountain, to a pleasant city, the roofs of which he could already see. The other was a rough mountain road, which looked very hard to climb. This one led up, up, up, for a long distance, growing rougher and rougher as it ascended the mountain, till it was lost to sight in the clouds.

As Hercules stood trying to make up his mind which road to choose, he saw a young woman coming slowly up the one which led to the city. Her gown was covered with embroidered flowers of all colours, and she wore a wreath of withered roses in her hair.

When she reached the place where Hercules stood, she saw that he was in doubt about the two roads, and eagerly advised him to take the smooth one which led so quickly to the city.

"In that city," said she, "you will find pleasant people, who will freely give you everything that you could possibly wish for. You need not work in the dust nor in the heat of the sun; but you may sit all day in pleasant gardens, where you will hear fountains splashing and birds singing, or where, if you prefer, you may listen to the music of the lyre."

As Hercules looked toward the city, the sound of music came to him, faintly, carried by the fresh morning breeze; and the gardens, with their trees and flowering shrubs, which surrounded each of the houses, looked so cool and inviting that he felt inclined to follow the young woman's advice. Still, something held him back.

Just then, he saw some one standing in the mountain road. This was a young woman too, but she looked very different from the first one. She wore plain white garments, and her eyes were sad, but brave.

"I will tell you the truth, Hercules," she said. "My sister is deceiving you. The pleasant things that they will offer you in that city on the plains below us are either not worth the having, or in the end you must pay a price for them of which you little dream. Do not go to that city, but come up the mountain road with me. The mountain road is hard to climb, and as you go higher, it will grow harder and harder, but you will have delights of which you can never tire. You will get the mountain air into your lungs, and this and the hard climbing will make a man of you. If you have the courage to climb high enough, this mountain road will lead you to Mount Olympus at last, and there you shall live forever with the gods, who cannot die." In his dream Hercules was wise, and chose the mountain road.

Not long after this, the real work of his life began, when he presented himself at the court of King Eurystheus, ready for any task that the king might have for him to do. Hercules, having been born somewhat later than his cousin Eurystheus, the king of Mycenæ, it became his fate to be the slave of this cousin.

There was nothing the Greeks admired more than great bodily strength. Hercules was already remarkable for his broad shoulders, and the large muscles of his arms, while Eurystheus, although a king, had always been weak and sickly.

Therefore, when Hercules stood before him for the first time, King Eurystheus looked at his strong young cousin, and felt his courage sink at the difference between this cousin and himself. Then an angry frown came over his face, and he resolved to set Hercules the hardest and most dangerous tasks that he could possibly contrive.

These tasks which Hercules performed for King Eurystheus became famous in after days, and were called the Twelve Labours of Hercules. Each one was a little harder than the last, and carried Hercules a little farther from home and a little nearer to the unknown western land, till in the twelfth he even reached the gates of Hades, where Pluto reigned.

III

THE FIRST LABOUR

The Strangling of the Nemean Lion

Near the sacred grove which surrounded the temple of Jupiter in Nemea, a fierce lion, called the Nemean lion, had its den. This lion was laying waste the country all about the valley of Nemea, and the people of that country lived in constant terror of its ravages. It went out every night, and sometimes by day, and killed hundreds of cattle or sheep, and occasionally took a man or a child, if any were foolhardy enough to come within its reach.

Eurystheus thought it would be an excellent plan to send Hercules to kill the Nemean lion. So he assigned this for his cousin's first task.

Without having any very definite idea of how he was to accomplish the task, the young hero took his bow and arrows, and started out. At the foot of Mount Helicon he found a wild olive tree, one that had grown slowly in stony soil, and was tough of fibre and full of knots. Instead of lopping off a branch for his purpose, as a weaker man might have done, Hercules pulled up this whole tree by the roots, and made a stout club of it. Then he went to the Nemean valley.

Not a herdsman nor a shepherd was in sight of whom he could inquire about the beast; for they were all afraid of it, and kept within doors, leaving their flocks to its mercy.

Hercules watched, near the temple, all day long. Toward night the lion came home to its lair. It looked very fierce and terrible. Its mane was all dashed with blood, and it was licking fresh blood from its chin. Hiding himself among some bushes, Hercules fixed an arrow into his bow. When the lion came near enough, he sent the arrow, singing, straight to its flank, but it glanced away, and fell on the grass. The lion paused in its slow walk, looked to the right and the left, and showed its teeth. Then Hercules shot another arrow, but this one glanced away like the first; for this was no common lion, and its skin was very tough. Hercules was making ready to shoot a third time, when the lion saw him. It lashed its tail, then crouched and sprang. Hercules met it with his club, and broke the club on its head, but stunned it in doing so. Then he seized its neck with both hands, and succeeded in strangling it, as he had strangled the snakes, when he was only a baby, in his shield-cradle. So ended the first of the twelve labours of Hercules.

When Hercules went back to King Eurystheus, he wore the skin of the Nemean lion over his shoulders, with the head of the beast resting on his own head like a kind of helmet. Eurystheus would hardly have been more frightened if he had suddenly seen the Nemean lion itself walking into his palace.

Hercules soon made himself another club, and after this he was seldom seen without both his club and his lion's skin.

IV

THE SECOND LABOUR

The Killing of the Lernean Hydra

The second labour that King Eurystheus planned for Hercules, made the slaying of a lion seem like child's play; for, Hercules having proved himself to be so brave and strong, the king sent him to kill the Lernean hydra.

This was a water-snake with nine heads, of which one was immortal, and therefore could not possibly be killed. It was so very poisonous that even the air from the marshes which it haunted often killed people. Its den was near the Fountain of Amymone. This prevented the peasants who lived in that region from making use of the water of the fountain. As the summers were long and dry in Argolis, and the springs and fountains few, this, too, was a very serious matter.

The twin brother of Hercules had a son, named Iolaus. When Hercules went to kill the Lernean hydra, he took Iolaus with him, that the boy might learn the ways of hunters.

After a long, dusty walk over the country roads, Hercules and Iolaus reached the Fountain of Amymone; and there, the first thing that they saw, was the hydra, stretching its nine heads out of its den, and hissing an angry warning with every head.

A few arrows sent buzzing against it brought the snake out into the marsh, and then Hercules set to work cutting off its heads with his sword. But for every head he cut off, two new ones grew, and the new heads began hissing and biting even more fiercely than the heads that had been cut off. Then, while the fight was going on, a crab came out and seized Hercules by the heel. This was altogether too much to contend with. Hercules saw that he must try a different plan. So he called to Iolaus to set fire to a grove of young trees that grew near the swamp, and to keep him supplied with burning brands. Iolaus did so.

Then Hercules, as he cut off a head, seared the stump, until only one was left. This, being the immortal head, would not burn. Hercules had cut it off, but as it lay in the grass, it spit venom more fiercely than ever. So Hercules rolled a huge rock over it, and thus prevented it from doing any more harm.

The fight being over, Hercules dipped his arrows in the poison of the hydra, which made them very dangerous weapons, and very unsafe ones to handle. The time came when he had reason to regret having meddled with this terrible poison.

V

THE THIRD LABOUR

The Capture of the Erymanthian Boar

King Eurystheus next sent Hercules to catch a wild boar that lived on Mount Erymanthus. Eurystheus told Hercules to catch the boar and bring it to Mycenæ alive; for he began to think that Hercules would succeed in killing almost any dangerous beast, but knew that the task of taking such a creature alive would be a much harder one.

Mount Erymanthus was in Arcadia. This was the first time that the labours of Hercules had taken him out of Argolis.

On his way to Mount Erymanthus, Hercules paid a visit to his friend Pholo, the centaur, who lived in a cave on that mountain. In Pholo's cave was a large vase of very choice wine. It did not belong to Pholo, alone, but was the common property of all the centaurs that lived on the mountain. It was the gift of the wine-god, Bacchus, who had told Pholo not to open it until Hercules should come to his cave. Now that Hercules had come, Pholo thought it right to open the wine-vase, without consulting the other centaurs. But the centaurs were a very rough, wild race of beings, and when they smelled the wine, which was so strong that its fumes spread all through the forest, they armed themselves with pine branches, rocks, torches, axes—whatever they could pick up most quickly—and came rushing into Pholo's cave. Seeing Hercules, and not knowing who he was or why he was there, they attacked him without waiting for any explanation.

Hercules had his quiver full of poisoned arrows, and was obliged to use them in self-defence. He succeeded in driving the centaurs away; but after they were gone, the friendly centaur, Pholo, picked up one of the arrows, and while he was looking at it curiously, let it slip from his hand and drop on his foot. The wound it made was as bad as a snake-bite, and poor Pholo soon died. This was the first time that Hercules wished he had not dipped his arrows in the poison of the hydra, but it was not the last.

After this, Hercules went on up the mountain, caught the Erymanthian boar, and brought it back on his shoulders to Mycenæ, alive.

Eurystheus was watching. When he saw Hercules coming over the plains, with the boar on his shoulders, he was badly frightened, and ran into his palace and hid himself. Just inside the palace doors stood a large bronze pot, with a cover. In his haste, Eurystheus jumped into this, and pulled the cover down over his head.

But he was not quite quick enough. Hercules came into the palace just then and caught a glimpse of Eurystheus just as the cover of the bronze pot was closing over him. Hercules pretended to see nothing, however; but remarking gravely to some nobles who were standing about, that the bronze pot would surely be the safest place in which to keep the boar, he quickly lifted the cover and popped it in.

You might think that this would be the end of King Eurystheus and his hard tasks. But, on the contrary, the king suffered no harm from his strange fellow-prisoner, who cowered down in the dark as frightened as the king himself.

This was the end of the third labour.

VI

THE FOURTH LABOUR

The Capture of Diana's Stag

After King Eurystheus had been pulled out of the bronze pot, and was seated upon his throne again, he set his wits to work to think of something really hard for Hercules to do.

In the great forests which lay on the borders of Arcadia roamed a very fleet stag. This stag had often befooled the hunters of that region. Very few had ever really seen it, and many people, perhaps King Eurystheus himself, believed that it lived only in hunters' stories. If these stories were to be believed, it had horns of gold and hoofs of brass; could take the most wonderful leaps; and was never tired, no matter how long the dogs had been chasing it. It had been seen browsing, oftener than anywhere else, close to the steps of Diana's temple; and many people believed that it was under her protection.

For the fourth labour, Eurystheus told Hercules to catch this stag and bring it back alive.

So Hercules went to the Arcadian forests, and hiding himself in the undergrowth, watched all the paths near the temple of Diana. It was tiresome watching. Flies stung him; bright-eyed lizards ran over his feet; and a little owl came and hooted among

the shadows of the temple. At last he saw the
golden-antlered stag, and the sight of it was worth
his long watch. He had never seen a more beautiful
animal. It had great soft eyes, and its golden antlers
seemed like a wonderful crown.

Hercules knew that he might never get another
sight of this elusive creature, so as soon as he saw it,
he darted out of his hiding-place and began the
chase.

The stag led him through the forest and over the
hills, across great rivers, and beyond the borders of
Arcadia. Still it kept on, never tiring, and Hercules
followed close behind it. The stag had never been
pursued before by a foe that showed such endurance.
On and on it went, with Hercules coming after, till
the chase had lasted a whole year, when it began to
show signs of fatigue.

It had led Hercules over nearly the whole of
Europe, in a great circle, and now it brought him
back to Diana's temple again. Panting and exhausted,
it ran into the temple. Hercules followed, and would
have caught it even in that spot, which was sacred
to Diana, but just then the moon burst out from a
dark cloud, and, looking up, Hercules suddenly saw
Diana herself standing before him. She looked very
tall, and her crown was like the new moon. At her
feet crouched the stag, trembling. Diana said to
Hercules: "You must not lay hands on this stag, as it

belongs to me; but go back to King Eurystheus and merely tell him all that has happened, and he will consider that your fourth labour is accomplished."

VII

THE FIFTH LABOUR

The Destruction of the Stymphalian Birds

King Eurystheus now sent Hercules to drive away the Stymphalian Birds.

The valley of Stymphalus was often visited by enormous flocks of strange birds. These birds did great damage to the crops and to the herds, for it was an easy matter for them to kill a sheep or a cow and feed on the carcass. Besides, they had been known to carry off children. These birds had sharp claws of iron, and feathers which were sharp at the quill end like the point of an arrow, and which they had the power of throwing at their enemies, as the porcupine was supposed to throw its quills. Of course these birds must have been a thousand times worse than any porcupine, because they could fly through the air, and throw their feathers from above. Their nests were in a thick, dark wood, in the midst of which was a pool.

Instead of trying to fight birds like these with his bow and arrows, or his club, or his hunting spears,

Hercules thought of another plan. He went quietly to the edge of the pool, and holding his bronze shield above his head to protect himself from the birds' feathers, he rang a large bell, and at the same time beat upon the shield with his lance.

The birds, frightened at the sudden clattering noise, flew up in such numbers that it seemed as if a great dark cloud had come over the sky. As they flew over the head of Hercules, their sharp feathers fell fast, rattling on the shield, and tearing the leaves of the surrounding trees into strips.

Hercules kept on ringing the bell and beating the shield till every bird had left the wood, except a half-dozen that had stayed behind to watch from the tops of the tallest trees. These few that were left, he easily shot with his poisoned arrows.

After this the birds built their nests on the Island of Mars, and never came back to trouble the valley of Stymphalus.

VIII

THE SIXTH LABOUR

The Cleaning of the Augean Stables

The next labour of Hercules was the cleaning of the Augean stables. King Eurystheus told him that he must do this work alone, and do it in one day.

King Augeas was a son of Helios, and one of the

heroes who sailed with Jason on the Quest of the
Golden Fleece. He was a king of Elis. His herds were
so large that, toward sundown, when the cattle came
up to the stables from their pastures, they seemed to
pour across the plains endlessly, as the fleecy white
clouds, driven by the west wind, sometimes roll
across the sky.

Among these cattle were twelve snow-white bulls,
which were sacred to Helios. One of them, the leader,
was so very white that he shone among the other
cattle, like a star, and had been named Phaethon,
after the son of Helios. When wild beasts—panthers
or wolves or even lions—came down from the
mountains to attack the herds, as they often did, the
twelve white bulls always went first to drive them
back, lowering their curly foreheads, shaking their
sharp horns, and bellowing, as they went, in a way to
frighten any beast that ever roamed the plains.

When Hercules went among the cattle of Augeas,
he wore his lion's skin as usual. The wind brought
the scent of the skin to Phaethon, who, connecting
that scent with the worst of the enemies from which
it was his duty to defend the herd, came rushing up
to attack Hercules. But Hercules, being so exceed-
ingly strong, had no fear of the bull; he simply caught
him by one white horn, turned his head and bent it
to the ground, showing himself to be the master.
After this, whenever Hercules came near, Phaethon

stood off respectfully, and the other cattle followed his example.

The stables of Augeas stood in a long line, close to the bank of a river. Hercules made quick work of this labour, for since the stables must be cleaned in one day, he dug a trench and turned the river through them. Numerous as the stables were, the running water soon swept them clean.

IX

THE SEVENTH LABOUR

The Capture of the Cretan Bull

When Minos was chosen king of Crete, he wished to begin his reign by offering a sacrifice to Jupiter. Accordingly, he went down to the seashore, and built an altar of rough stones. Then he called on the sea-god, Neptune, asking him to send an animal for the sacrifice. He had scarcely expressed this desire, before there rose up out of the sea, a snow-white bull with silvery horns. There could not have been a more beautiful animal, or one more perfect for a sacrifice; but Minos thought it a pity that he could not keep such a superb creature, and when he found that it was gentle, as well as perfect in every other respect, instead of sacrificing it on the altar that he had built, he led it to the pasture where his own herd were feeding, and let it go.

This was wrong, because Neptune had sent the bull to be sacrificed to Jupiter, and for no other purpose. Therefore, the gods caused the beautiful creature to lose its gentle disposition, and to become wild and dangerous. It roamed through the woods of Crete, and was a terror to every one who lived on that island.

At last, King Eurystheus sent Hercules, for his seventh labour, to capture this Cretan bull.

Armed only with his club, Hercules went into a wood where the bull had been oftenest seen, and waited by a spring. Soon he heard a hoarse bellowing, and caught a glimpse of something white, through the trees. A moment later, he saw the animal coming up to attack him and tossing its white horns fiercely. Throwing his club to the ground, he caught the bull by the horns, and held it firmly, in spite of its struggles, for he was the stronger of the two.

When the bull saw that it had found its master, its former gentle disposition returned to it, and it forgot all its wild ways, and followed Hercules about as if it had been a pet lamb. Afterward, in taking it to Mycenæ, Hercules let it swim across the sea, while he rode on its back.

X

THE EIGHTH LABOUR

The Capture of the Horses of Diomedes

Diomedes, a king of Thrace, was a fierce, war-loving monarch, who was said to be a son of Mars. He had no regard for the laws of hospitality. When people were wrecked on his coasts, they were seldom heard from again.

He had a pair of war-horses, so vicious and dangerous that they had to be fastened with chains. It was whispered that the reason why the horses of Diomedes were so very dangerous was that they were fed on human flesh; and furthermore, that this explained the complete disappearance of all who had been wrecked on the coasts of King Diomedes.

King Eurystheus sent Hercules to bring the horses of Diomedes to Mycenæ, and as usual, to make the task harder, he desired him to bring them alive.

Hercules went to the country of Diomedes, and here he soon found that the dreadful reports he had heard about this ruler were all true. He went straight to the king's stables, and easily overpowered the guards. Then he unfastened the horses, fierce as they were, and led them by their chains to the shore. But here he was overtaken by a crowd of angry men, all calling upon him to stop.

He soon found himself fighting with King Diomedes himself. This strange king liked nothing better than fighting, and fully intended that Hercules should furnish a meal for his horses. But Hercules soon overpowered the king and made him a prisoner, thus putting an end to his cruelty.

Then Hercules took the horses to Mycenæ, and presented them to King Eurystheus, who doubtless was delighted at receiving such a valuable present. The horses soon escaped from his stables, and ran wild in the Arcadian hills, where they were finally eaten by wolves.

XI

THE NINTH LABOUR

The Securing of the Girdle of Hippolyte

Soon after the capture of the horses of Diomedes, Hercules was sent to the country of the Amazons to get Queen Hippolyte's girdle.

The Amazons were a race of women who delighted in warfare and hunting. They lived at some distance from Greece, on the Caucasus Mountains and on the borders of the Black Sea. Their queen, Hippolyte, had a very famous girdle, which was a gift to her from Mars, the war-god. It was said to be some magic power in this girdle which made the onslaught of the Amazons so like a rushing, irresistible storm.

The Greeks, in their wars, had more than once found themselves opposed to the Amazons, and knew them for a formidable enemy.

The daughter of Eurystheus, who was a priestess, thought that Hercules could not do a better service for the Greeks than to secure this girdle of Queen Hippolyte. So Eurystheus sent him for it.

Hercules, therefore, crossed the Black Sea, and went to the country of the Amazons. He anchored his ship in the harbour, not far from the queen's palace, and Queen Hippolyte and some of her women went on board, to see who had come among them. The queen, who was brave herself, and admired courage in others, welcomed the famous Hercules in a kindly manner, and gave him the girdle. But one of the Amazons, seeing the queen on board the ship, raised the cry that a stranger was carrying off Queen Hippolyte by force. The Amazons then armed themselves and flew toward the ship from all directions. In spite of this, Hercules escaped with the girdle,—although not without fighting,—and was soon crossing the Black Sea on his way home.

When he reached Mycenæ, he presented the famous girdle, which was set with precious stones and heavy with gold, to the daughter of King Eurystheus. So ended his ninth labour.

XII

THE TENTH LABOUR

The Fetching of the Cattle of Geryon

You would think that all the monsters in the neighbourhood of Mycenæ must have been slain by this time, and all the near-by kings and queens who were enemies of King Eurystheus, overcome. In fact, Eurystheus did find it necessary to send Hercules a long distance from Mycenæ, next time; for he ordered him to go to an island that lay just beyond the country where the sun sets, and bring back the red cattle of the giant, Geryon.

This Geryon was a most extraordinary giant. He had three bodies, three heads, six legs, and six arms, besides a pair of wings. He had an enormous herd of cattle, which he kept, at night, in a dark cave.

To aid him in this tenth labour, Hercules borrowed the golden cup in which the sun-god, Helios, was borne round the world, from west to east, every night. This cup would float on the water like a boat, and had the remarkable power of becoming larger or smaller, according to the needs of the person using it. In it Hercules was carried straight west for a long time—farther west than any one had ever gone before.

Oceanus, the god of the ocean, was angry at having his dominions invaded, and raised a great storm.

The golden cup was caught in a whirling cloud of spray, and tossed up and down as if it had been a bubble. But Hercules, nothing daunted, aimed one of his arrows at Oceanus, who laughed heartily at this impertinence, and then quieted the waters.

When Hercules reached the island, he climbed a high mountain, in order that he might look out over all the land, and see where the cattle of Geryon were grazing. As he stood there he was attacked by Geryon's savage two-headed dog. He killed the beast with his club, but hardly had time to draw a long breath before he was attacked by Geryon's herdsman, who was quite as savage as the dog, and would gladly have torn Hercules limb from limb. With a single blow from his ponderous club, he killed the herdsman also.

Then he saw the cattle grazing in a meadow, and began to drive them away. By this time Geryon himself had seen him, and came striding toward him swinging six clubs at a time with his six hands, and bellowing threats of death and destruction from all three of his huge throats at once. He looked like an animated windmill as he came down the hill, and would have frightened most people out of their wits. But Hercules remembered his poisoned arrows, and he sent a shaft so straight, that it made an end of the giant before he came near enough to do any harm.

Then Hercules gathered the cattle together and

drove them into the cup of Helios, in which he transported them to the mainland. Afterward, some of them died, having been attacked by enormous swarms of flies; and others were lost through meeting with robbers and giants, but he succeeded in driving the remainder all the way to Mycenæ.

XIII
THE ELEVENTH LABOUR
The Procuring of the Golden Apples

After Hercules brought the cattle of Geryon to Mycenæ, King Eurystheus, wishing the hero farther away than ever, sent him once more to the country beyond the sunset. This time the king's excuse was, that he wished to have three of the golden apples which grew in the Garden of the Hesperides.

Although all had heard of this famous garden, no one at Mycenæ could tell Hercules where to find it. Some said it was far to the north, others that it was far to the west.

So Hercules started out, and walked in a north-westerly direction, till he reached the river Rhone.

There he found the river-nymphs playing among the rocks. They told him that Nereus, the sea-god, knew where to find the Garden of the Hesperides, but would never tell the secret unless he were compelled to do so. They told him also that, without any fear of what might happen, he must seize Nereus, and hold him fast till he gave the desired information.

Thanking the nymphs for their kindness, Hercules followed the Rhone down to the place where it flowed into the sea. Then he lay in wait behind some rocks, till the sun went down and the moon came up.

Presently, a queer little old man came up out of the water, and set about making himself comfortable for a nap on shore. The old man had short horns growing from his forehead, and his long hair and beard had the appearance of a tangle of seaweed. Hercules knew at once that this was Nereus; and as soon as he saw the poor old sea-god sleeping soundly, he ran out and seized him, as the nymphs had said he must.

All at once he found that he was holding a struggling stag; then the stag became a sea-bird, screaming to get free; the sea-bird changed to a fierce three-headed dog; the three-headed dog took the form of the giant, Geryon, who seemed to have come to life again, and to be more savage than ever; next Geryon changed to a monstrous snake. All this time Hercules held on tighter and tighter. At last, Nereus, seeing that he could not frighten Hercules into letting him go, took his proper shape again and asked him what he wanted.

Hercules replied that he only wanted to know how to get three of the golden apples which grew in the Garden of the Hesperides. Nereus told him that if he would go down into Africa, where the giant Atlas was holding up the sky, Atlas would get the apples for him.

So Hercules went down into Africa. Almost as soon as he had touched the African shore, he was attacked by a terrible earth-born giant, called Antæus. This was a very difficult giant to conquer. The secret of his wonderful strength was that his mother Gæa, the goddess of the earth, made him stronger than ever, each time that he touched the ground. But Hercules, knowing how Gæa helped him, held him high above the earth, and so strangled him. It had been the habit of Antæus to kill all travellers who passed that way, but he never killed any more after meeting with Hercules.

When his fight with Antæus was over, Hercules lay down on the ground and went to sleep. He soon awoke, feeling as if he were being stung by a thousand insects. Sitting up, and rubbing his eyes, what should he see but a multitude of tiny people, no larger than bumble-bees, who, while he was asleep, had been climbing over his body, and attacking him with their little bows and arrows. These were the Pygmies. Hercules laughed heartily at their warfare, and then he tied a few of them into a corner of his lion's skin, to take to Eurystheus.

After this, he wandered about in Africa for a long time. At last he found Atlas. Seeing how tired the giant looked, Hercules offered to take the burden of the sky upon his own shoulders for a while, if Atlas would get him the three golden apples. This Atlas readily consented to do.

So Hercules held up the sky, while Atlas went to get the apples. This was an easy thing for Atlas to do, for the nymphs who kept the garden were his nieces.

When Atlas came back with the apples, as he did shortly, he himself offered to carry them to Eurystheus, if Hercules would only hold up the sky a little longer, and he meant that Hercules should continue to hold up the sky, forever.

But Hercules saw through the trick, and matched it with another. He thanked Atlas, and asked him to take the sky again, for a moment, while he found a pad which would make the weight much easier to bear. So Atlas took the sky again. Then Hercules took the apples, and although Atlas shouted to him to come back, he was soon beyond the sound of the giant's voice, and well on his way to Mycenæ.

XIV

THE TWELFTH LABOUR

The Bringing of Cerberus from the Underworld

Hercules had now accomplished eleven out of his twelve labours. If he succeeded once more, Eurystheus would be obliged to set him free.

The twelfth labour was the most difficult and dangerous of all. It was nothing less than to go down into Pluto's kingdom and bring back to Mycenæ Pluto's three-headed watch-dog, Cerberus.

No doubt, Eurystheus thought that this would be impossible, and that he should never have to set Hercules free; or that, if the hero were foolish enough to go down into Pluto's kingdom, he would never be seen or heard from again.

In a certain dark, gloomy grove, even farther to the west than the Garden of the Hesperides, was a chasm between two huge rocks. Down very deep in this chasm, if one had the hardihood to look in, one might see the faint sparkle of water—water that looked as black as ink. A strange and very unpleasant odour, a kind of sulphurous smell, hung about the spot. If wild birds flew over that black water, they wavered in their flight for an instant, then fell headlong into the chasm, and never came out again. Strange rumblings were sometimes heard there. It was one of the places through which Pluto's kingdom, the great gloomy underworld, could be entered. The underworld could be entered here, but no one who went down into that black hole had ever been known to come back.

However, Hercules had never been afraid of anything yet, and he was not afraid to go down into this chasm. Down he went, armed only with his club, his

bow and arrows, and his lion's skin. He clambered
down the rocks till he had reached a great depth,
then he walked through a long, dark passage till he
came to a gate. There, by a very faint light, which
came from a cleft in the mountains above, he saw
Cerberus with his three savage heads, and his snake's
tail, guarding the way.

When the dog saw Hercules, instead of growling
and bristling, he wagged his horrid tail, and came
forward as if he meant to welcome him to his master's
kingdom.

Hercules passed in at the gate, and as he did so, a
great number of shadowy ghosts, that had been
looking out from between the bars, fluttered away,
like so many bats.

Hercules kept on, walking through dark caves and
narrow passages, till he came to Pluto's throne. Then
he told Pluto, frankly, what the order of Eurystheus
had been, and asked the privilege of taking Cerberus
back with him to Mycenæ. Since Hercules had done
and suffered so much, and had proved himself a
true hero, Pluto granted him this privilege, but only
on the condition that he should capture the dog
without the use of weapons of any kind.

So Hercules went back to the gate. There was
Cerberus. But instead of fawning on him as he had
done before, the dog was now very fierce, showing
his teeth, and bristling, and looking formidable,

indeed. Still, Hercules was not afraid. He seized
Cerberus quickly, and overpowered him, with the
vice-like grip of his hands. King Eurystheus almost
tumbled off his throne, when he saw Hercules come
back from the underworld, actually dragging Cerberus
after him. He could hardly believe his own eyes. He
now set his cousin free, because he could not do
otherwise; but he immediately forbade him to enter
again the gates of Mycenæ, as he thought that this
powerful cousin might take his kingdom from him.
Hercules, however, had no such intention.

XV

THE ASCENT TO MOUNT OLYMPUS

By this time, all the neighbouring kingdoms rang
with the fame of Hercules. Now that he was no
longer obliged to work for King Eurystheus, every
king or noble, who was at war with his neighbours,
or who was troubled with robbers or wild beasts in
his own dominions, applied to him for help.

So there was still plenty to do. In fact, Hercules
gave himself no rest, for he listened to every appeal,
feeling that it was the work of his life to rid the world
of all monstrous evils.

At last the time came when he was taken up to
Mount Olympus to live with the gods, as the wise
man, Tiresias, had foretold.

It happened in this way. Hercules, as was befitting for such a hero, married a king's daughter. When he was taking home his bride, whose name was Deianeira, he came to a swollen river. As he stood on the bank, wondering how he could cross, a centaur came galloping up, and offered to carry Deianeira across on his back. Hercules accepted the offer. When the river was crossed, the centaur, with Deianeira still on his back, started off across the hills, running swiftly, for he meant to steal the bride.

Hercules called to him to come back; then, as he only ran away the more swiftly, sent one of his poisoned arrows after him. The centaur fell to the ground with the poison of the hydra spreading through his veins. As he lay dying, he gave Deianeira a charm, which, he said, should she ever lose her husband's love, would have the power to bring it back. In reality, this charm was a deadly poison, for it had been dipped in the centaur's blood, which was filled with the venom of the hydra.

For many years after this Hercules and his wife lived happily together, and Deianeira almost forgot about the centaur and his charm. But one day she became madly jealous.

At this time Hercules was on Mount Œta, where he had built an altar of rough stones. He was making preparations for a sacrifice. When everything was ready, he sent a messenger to Deianeira for his sacrificial robe.

Deianeira took the robe from the chest where it had been carefully laid away; and as she unfolded it, admiring its rich embroidery, which had been worked by her own hands a long time before, a small package fell from its folds to the floor. It was the centaur's charm.

"Oh, the centaur knew that I should need this one day," she said to herself. "Now I will win back the love of Hercules."

Then, entirely ignorant of the fact that she was using a powerful poison, Deianeira heated water in a kettle, put into it the contents of the package, and steeped the robe in the preparation thus made. As soon as it could be dried, she sent it to Hercules.

It seemed to Hercules that the messenger kept him waiting a long time. When the robe was brought at last, it had a queer look and a disagreeable odour, which reminded him of something, he could not remember what.

But it was getting late, so he took the robe hastily, and threw it over his shoulders. Instantly he felt as if he were enveloped in fire. Not knowing what he was doing, he threw down the altar, uprooted great trees, and seizing the messenger, hurled him over the top of Mount Œta into the sea.

When the torture of the poison began to grow less, Hercules realized that this was the end of all his labours. He made a funeral pile of the great trees that he had torn up in his agony, mounted it, spread out his lion's skin, and lay down with his head resting on his club.

Meanwhile his friends, seeing the commotion on Mount Œta, came to see what had happened. Hercules requested one of these friends—the one who had always been nearest to him—to set fire to the pile. With great sorrow this friend stepped forward and touched a burning torch to the logs.

Then a wonderful thing happened. Have you ever seen a serpent that had just cast its old, faded skin, and had come out in glossy new scales? A change like this came to Hercules.

For all those labours that he had accomplished, and all the suffering that he had passed through had developed in him a strong and courageous spirit, which could not die, but was immortal. All that could die was burned to ashes. But the immortal Hercules, the real Hercules, came out from the fire all shining and glorious.

Then a rainbow appeared in the sky. It was Iris's bridge. A moment after, the clouds overhead broke away, and Iris in all her shimmering colours, and Mercury with his winged shoes, came lightly down the rainbow bridge from heaven to earth.

They led the immortal Hercules, the shining new Hercules, to Mount Olympus, to live forever among the gods, with all who are truly brave.

29

Theseus

I

HOW THESEUS CAME TO ATHENS

THESEUS, and his mother Æthra lived at the foot of a great lonesome mountain, at a place called Trœzen. One day, long before the earliest time that Theseus could remember, Ægeus, the father of Theseus, took Æthra out among the singing pines on the mountain side. There he lifted a huge rock, and buried underneath it his sword and sandals. Then rolling the rock back into its place, he told Æthra that when Theseus was strong enough to lift this rock, she might let him take the sword and sandals and go to his father at Athens. This was the last that Æthra had ever seen of Ægeus, but she knew that he was the king of Attica, and sat on the throne in the beautiful city of Athens.

At last the time came when Theseus had reached a man's full strength, and could lift the great rock. Then taking the sword and the sandals from under it, he fastened the sword at his side, put the sandals on his feet, and was soon ready to set out for Athens.

At that time the country between Trœzen and Athens was wild and rocky, and behind many of the rocks lurked giants and robbers, ready to spring out upon lonely travellers; but by sea, the way was much safer. Æthra's father, who was getting old and feeble, thought that Theseus had better go by sea, but Theseus said, "No! Have I not my father's good sword? I will go by land, and if I meet with any adventures, so much the better."

So Theseus bade good-bye to his mother and his grandfather, and began his journey by land. He had not gone far among the wild rocks and crags near to Trœzen, before he was attacked by the robber, Periphetes, who was called the club-bearer. This robber came running toward Theseus, swinging a great iron club. He looked very terrible indeed; but Theseus, with his father's sword in his hand, went bravely forward, and soon left the club-bearer lying dead in the road. The way to Athens was now so much the safer. Theseus took the great iron club of Periphetes and went on.

Next, he met with the pine-bender, a giant named Sinis, who used to catch all the travellers passing his way, and tear them to pieces. The pine-bender did this by bending down the tops of two pine trees and then letting them spring back again, after having tied his captives between them. Sinis carried a young pine tree for a club. Enormous as this club was, it was not so strong as the iron one which Theseus now carried.. So when Sinis tried to tie Theseus to the tops of two pines, he found that he had met his match; for the iron club of Theseus came crashing down on the pine-tree club of Sinis, and splintered it into shreds. Then a blow or two more stretched the giant out under his pines.

Before Theseus had gone very much farther on the road to Athens, he came to a village where all the people were living in terror of a fierce wild boar. He found this animal and killed it.

Then he went on till he came to the shore of a gulf, where the robber, Sciron, lived. Sciron had a strange way of showing hospitality to travellers. After inviting them to remain overnight at his house, he used to seat himself on the edge of a high cliff, and set his guests to washing his feet. While they were engaged in this work, he would kick them off the cliff into the sea. But he never did this again after Theseus travelled that road; for Theseus threw Sciron himself over the same cliff.

Not far away lived another robber, Procrustes, who used to pretend to entertain strangers at his hut. Then, if they were too long for his bedstead, he would cut off their heads or their feet; if they were too short for it, he would stretch them to fit it.

Procrustes, too, was slain by Theseus. Afterward other robbers and giants met the same fate.

By the time that Theseus reached Athens, he was well known in that city; for the people all along the way had been eager to spread the news of what he had done. In fact, only one man in all Athens knew nothing of his coming, and that man was his own father, Ægeus, the king.

At this time Medea, a beautiful woman and a famous sorceress, was living in the king's palace. As she had a son whom she wished to place on the throne after King Ægeus was gone, perhaps it was natural that she should be sorry to have Theseus come to Athens. But this perfectly natural feeling of Medea's led to a very wicked act.

By means of her knowledge of poisonous herbs she mixed a very powerful cup, which would cause instant death to any one who drank of it. Then, telling King Ægeus that the young stranger was a traitor, and had plotted against his life, she contrived to make him hand this cup to Theseus, when he presented himself at the throne.

With no thought that it could contain poison, Theseus innocently raised the fatal cup to his lips, intending to drink to the king. Just then Ægeus noticed the sword Theseus carried, and he knew by the carving on its ivory hilt that the so-called traitor was his own son. Instantly, he struck the cup from the hand of Theseus, and welcomed the young man as a father should welcome his son.

When Medea saw that her wicked scheme had miscarried, and that Theseus was recognized by his father, she was frightened. She did not dare to plan any further mischief to Theseus, but used all her enchantments to get herself safely away. First, she compelled a thick mist to rise from the river. Then, in the sudden darkness and confusion caused by the mist, she called her winged dragons, jumped into her chariot, and was soon far away from Athens, whither she never dared to return.

The people lost no time in telling the king all the brave deeds that Theseus had performed on his way from Trœzen. The king was so well pleased with what he heard, and so glad to have his son come to Athens, that he appointed three days of public rejoicing and feasting. In the midst of all this merrymaking, a messenger came to tell King Ægeus that the collectors of the tribute had arrived from Crete.

A long time before, the oldest son of King Minos of Crete had been slain in Athens. To avenge the death of the prince, King Minos brought a great army against Athens, and compelled the Athenians to pay him a tribute every ninth year, of seven young men and seven maidens, chosen from among the noble families of Athens. It was whispered that the children of the tribute, as these young men and maidens were called, were destined to be devoured by the Minotaur, a bloodthirsty and savage creature, with the body of a man and the head of a bull, which King Minos kept in a labyrinth near his palace. No one who entered the labyrinth had ever been known to come out again. The cruel tribute had been paid twice already, and now the Athenians must pay it for the third time.

Theseus at once resolved to kill the monstrous Minotaur, and so make an end of the tribute. Although King Ægeus tried to persuade him not to do so, he offered himself, before the lots were drawn, as one of the seven young men. This pleased the Athenians, and made Theseus very popular.

On the day appointed, the six other young men and the seven maidens were drawn by lot, and everything was made ready for sailing. When starting out on such a sad voyage, it seemed fitting that the ship which carried the children of the tribute should be rigged with black sails. This had been done on the two former occasions when the tribute had been paid. Now that there was some hope of a happy outcome of the voyage, King Ægeus gave Theseus a white sail, which he told him to hoist instead of the black one, if he should succeed in killing the Minotaur, and should start out on the homeward voyage safe and well. The aged king then bade his son good-bye, and said to him, "From the top of yonder rock I shall watch every day for your return."

Then the black-sailed ship passed slowly out of the harbour. The young people that it carried were very sad; for they never expected to see the sunny shores of Greece again, at least none of them but Theseus. He was as cheerful and as full of courage as when he set out for Athens with his father's sword hanging at his side.

II

THE SLAYING OF THE MINOTAUR

When the children of the tribute arrived at Crete, Theseus informed King Minos that he meant to kill the Minotaur. King Minos told the prince that if he could perform this task, he and all his companions might go free, and that nothing more should ever be said about the tribute.

The truth is, this horrible Minotaur was not altogether a pleasant pet to keep, for there was always the possibility that he might get out of the labyrinth and do no end of damage. Therefore King Minos would really have been very glad to get rid of him. Nevertheless, he was so hard-hearted that he would not permit Theseus to go armed to meet the monster; hence there was very little hope of the hero's success.

That night the young Athenians were thrown into

a dungeon under the palace of King Minos, one of them being destined for the Minotaur's breakfast in the morning.

Directly over this dungeon were the rooms of the two daughters of King Minos, Ariadne and Phædra. As the two sisters stood on the wall, enjoying the moonlight, they heard the complaining of the captives.

"What a pity it is," said Ariadne, "that these youths and maidens should become food for the Minotaur. I pity young Prince Theseus most of all, because he is so brave. If you are willing, we will help him to slay the Minotaur."

Phædra was as eager as Ariadne to help the young prince. So the two made a plan that they thought might succeed.

They waited till all the king's household were asleep, then stole softly to the dungeon, and opened the door. Worn out with fatigue and anxiety, all the captives but Theseus had fallen asleep. Theseus, however, was wide awake. Ariadne beckoned to him to come out. Then she and Phædra took him to the place where the famous labyrinth stood. Its white marble walls looked very high and strong in the moonlight. The night was very still, save for the lapping of the waves on the shore, and Theseus could distinctly hear the heavy breathing of the sleeping Minotaur.

"This is the best time to attack the creature; do not wait till morning," Ariadne whispered, and Theseus knew that she was right. "The Minotaur's den is in the very heart of the labyrinth," Ariadne continued. "The sound of his breathing will show you in what direction you must go. Here is a sword, and here is a clew of thread, by means of which, after you have killed the monster, you can find your way back." With these words she handed him the sword, and the clew or ball of thread, of which she kept the end in her own hand, then opened for him a door leading by a secret passage into the labyrinth.

Theseus, holding the sword in one hand and the clew in the other, entered the labyrinth. The interior was all cut up into narrow paths, bordered by high walls. So many of these paths ended in a blank wall that Theseus often had to retrace his steps. There never was another labyrinth half so intricate as this one, which was made by the famous Dædalus. Back and forth, in and out, Theseus went; he could hear the heavy breathing more and more plainly, and knew that he was getting nearer to the den of the monster he was seeking.

Meanwhile Ariadne and Phædra stood at the gate, Ariadne holding her end of the thread. They waited a long time—they could not tell how long. The moon set behind the hills, and left only the light of the stars. Then they heard a great roar that shook the strong walls of the labyrinth. After this everything was still again. It was hard for Ariadne to wait, now, for she did not know but Theseus might be lying dead inside, or, if he had not been killed by the Minotaur, might have dropped the thread in the fight, and so be lost in the maze of paths. At last she felt the thread tighten, and in a moment more out Theseus came, saying that he had slain the Minotaur.

Fortunately the galley that had brought Theseus and his companions to Crete was still lying on the shore. This made it possible to escape from King Minos before daylight. The sleeping youths and maidens in the dungeon were quickly roused, the little ship was launched, and all were soon ready to set out for Athens.

Before going aboard Theseus asked the daughters of King Minos to go with his companions and himself to Athens. "Your father, the king, will be angry," said he, "when he knows how you have aided me. This will be the best way to escape his wrath."

Having good reason to fear the cruelty of King Minos, the two princesses accepted this invitation.

On their way to Athens the young people stopped at the island of Naxos. Here, the young men, exhausted from hard rowing and greatly in need of rest, pulled the galley up on the shore, where the whole company encamped on the bare rocks for the

night. Very early the next morning they set sail, and
started off again; but Ariadne, being fast asleep on a
rock, was left behind.

When this poor princess awoke, she could hardly
believe that Theseus had really meant to desert her.
However, there was the galley dancing on the waves,
almost out of sight. She watched it till she could no
longer look off on the bright water because of the
tears in her eyes, and then she heard strange music,
a sound of tambourines and pipes, and the clash of
cymbals.

She turned to look toward the pine wood behind
her, from which the sounds came, and saw a chariot
drawn by two panthers. In the chariot sat Bacchus,
the god of the vine, wearing a spotted fawn-skin and
a crown of cool ivy-leaves. In coming through the
wood the god had twisted a spray of wild morning-
glory around his lance, and had thrust the sharp end
of the lance into a large pine-cone. He was surrounded
by a merry, dancing crowd of nymphs and satyrs.

When Bacchus heard Ariadne's story, he said:
"Theseus should certainly have taken you to Athens,
and considering all you did to help him, he ought,
at the very least, to have made you a queen. But never
mind, you shall have a better crown than any he
could have given you." With these words the god
placed a crown of nine bright stars on Ariadne's
head. After this he persuaded the other gods to take

her up into the sky, among themselves. There, in the northern sky, her crown still shines.

With all his courage Theseus must have been a very forgetful young man; for he not only left Ariadne on the island, but he forgot to hoist the white sail on the homeward voyage, as he had promised to do, if all went well. Thus it happened that the ship came back to Athens with the ominous black sail flying.

Poor old King Ægeus, watching from the rock, saw the black sail, and thinking that his son was dead, threw himself into the sea and was drowned. So when the children of the tribute arrived safe in the harbour after such a hazardous journey, there was mourning instead of rejoicing.

After Theseus was made king, he brought his mother, Æthra, to Athens, and took good care of her for the rest of her life. He ruled wisely, and was kind to the poor and the unfortunate.

30

Philemon and Baucis

IN a certain pleasant valley, surrounded by low mountains, there was once a very wicked village. Strangers who had passed through this village on their travels complained bitterly of the inhabitants. They said that as they passed along the road, if they were tired and hungry, and looked at the open doors of the houses, hoping for hospitality, it was only to see the doors slammed in their faces, and to hear the grinding of bolts. Not only this, but they had been stoned and ill-treated in every possible way. It was no wonder that the news of these things reached the gods of Olympus.

One day two strangers, who were somewhat different from travellers in general, passed through the place. It was almost dark, and the night air felt sharp and frosty. The strangers knocked at door after door, without finding any one who was willing to admit them, till they had tried every house but one in the village.

The last house of all stood out a little beyond the others, on the edge of a great swamp. It was a small cottage with only two rooms, and the roof was thatched with straw and with reeds from the swamp. Here lived two old people, Philemon and Baucis.

This old couple, who were not at all like the rest of the people in the village, would never have thought of throwing stones at strangers, of setting dogs on them, or of bolting their doors when they saw them coming. Instead of doing any of these things, they opened their doors, and invited the two strangers to come in.

The door of this modest little cottage was so low that the taller of the two strangers had to bend his head as he entered. Inside, the two rooms were almost bare of furniture. But Philemon and Baucis, poor as they were, made the strangers welcome to the best of all they had.

Baucis drew the ashes from the fire, which had been kept from the day before, brought in faggots, and soon had them crackling under a small kettle. While the water was heating, she brought vegetables from her little garden, and sat down to strip off the leaves.

Meanwhile, Philemon lifted down a side of bacon which hung on a beam overhead, and cut off a piece for Baucis to cook.

Then Baucis brought out a rickety table, blocked up one of the legs to make it stand level, and polished it off with a handful of fragrant mint. Next she placed upon the table a few figs that had grown in her own garden, a brown loaf, and a bottle of home-made wine, still sweet. When the bacon and the vegetables were done, she roasted some fresh eggs in the embers. The dinner was now ready, and the strangers were invited to seat themselves at the table.

If Philemon and Baucis had been alone, their dinner would have consisted of nothing more than the brown bread and the home-made wine, with perhaps a small scrap of bacon. But Baucis thought that the strangers must be tired and hungry, and besides, it seemed to her that it was her duty to show these chance guests such hospitality as her small means would allow.

Almost at the beginning of the meal a very strange thing happened. The cup of sweet wine, as it was passed round the table from one to another, was always full to the brim, no matter how much had just been drunk.

When Philemon and Baucis saw this, they were frightened. They had heard of such things happening, when people had been entertaining the gods, unawares. Looking at their guests more closely, they saw that the taller one certainly had a majestic air. The other had a face whose expression was constantly changing, and there was a look of mischief in his bright eyes.

The first thought of both of the old people, now, was that they had not done enough for such guests. Baucis jumped up from her chair, and ran out to catch the goose—the only thing that she and Philemon had left—intending to cook that, too. Philemon tried to help her, but neither of the old people could see very well, and they could not catch the goose. It raised its great white wings, and ran hither and thither. At last it ran into the cottage and straight up to the two strange guests, who said it should not be killed.

Then the guests told Philemon and Baucis who they were, and why they had come to the village. It was Jupiter and Mercury. They had heard the complaints of the travellers who had been so badly used, and had come to see whether the people of that village really were as wicked as they had been reported to be. They had found it all too true, and now, they said, these people must be punished.

Then they told the old couple, who had taken no share in the wickedness of the other villagers, to follow them up the mountain-side. There was a full moon, and Philemon and Baucis could see almost as clearly as their old eyes would let them see in the daytime. When they had nearly reached the top of the mountain, Jupiter told them to turn and look back at the village. The houses were slowly sinking out of sight, and presently a lake took their place, and looked as peaceful in the moonlight as if no village had ever been there. Not one of the village people was ever seen again.

Then a change came over the house of Philemon and Baucis. The thatched roof began to look yellow, like gold, while the sides grew white, and it became a marble temple, with a golden roof.

Jupiter told Philemon and Baucis to wish for whatever they liked, and their wish should be granted. The two old people could think of nothing better than that they might die at exactly the same moment, so that neither one should be left to mourn the other. Jupiter and Mercury then vanished and the old people went back down the mountain, and became priest and priestess in the temple, where they lived happily for many years.

One morning early, a long, long time afterward, some peasants came up to the temple with a present of new-laid eggs for the old priest and priestess. On coming near the temple what was their astonishment to see two grand old trees, an oak and a lime, standing just in front of the temple doors, where no tree had ever stood before. This was a marvel to them. When they came to look for Philemon and Baucis, they could not find them, and the two old people were never seen in that country again. But the two trees stood there for many,

many centuries, even after the temple had grown old and fallen to ruin. Travellers who rested in their hospitable shade, used to tell each other the story of the wicked villagers, and of Philemon and Baucis.

31

Orpheus and Eurydice

ORPHEUS, the son of Apollo, was a wonderful musician. He had a lyre of his own, and learned to play on it, when he was very young. This lyre was not quite so fine a one, perhaps, as Apollo's famous golden lyre, but it could produce marvellous music.

Orpheus often went to a lonely place, outside the village, where he would sit on the rocks and play all day long. Then the spiders stopped their spinning, the ants left off running to and fro, and the bees forgot to gather honey; for none of them had ever heard such sweet music before. The little birds who had their nests in the grass did not know what new singer had come among them. They gathered around Orpheus to listen, some hopping around on the rocks, and others swinging on tall weeds, and trying to catch the tune.

One day a cobra, gliding by slyly under the grass-heads, in the hope of finding eggs or young birds in some ground-nest, heard the music, and stopped to listen. He coiled himself up, raised his head, and swayed back and forth, in time to the music. The birds had nothing to fear from him while such music was filling the air. But they knew him well, as he lived close by under a rock.

As Orpheus grew older, his music became more and more wonderful. When he went to the old place to play, all the animals and birds in the fields and in the forest gathered around him. Lions, bears, wolves, foxes, eagles, hawks, owls, squirrels, little field-mice, and many other kinds of creatures were in the audience. Even the trees in the grove, near by, tore themselves up by the roots, and came and stood in the circle around Orpheus, so that they could hear better. Their branches cast a pleasant shade over the other listeners, and over Orpheus, as well, keeping off the hot rays of the afternoon sun.

The nymphs of the valley soon made friends with Orpheus, and when he had grown to be a man, one of them, whose name was Eurydice, became his wife.

One day, as Eurydice was running carelessly through the meadows, she stepped on the cobra that lived under the rock. Although the cobra was always gentle when under the influence of the magical music of Orpheus, he was not so at other times. He turned, instantly, and bit Eurydice on the ankle.

Then Eurydice had to go down to the dark underworld, where Pluto was king, and Proserpine queen.

When Orpheus came back to the meadows, he

could not find Eurydice. He took his lyre, and played his sweetest, most entrancing strains, while he wandered all about the mountains and valleys, calling to her. Her sister nymphs joined him in the search, and everywhere the hills echoed their calls of "Eurydice, Eurydice!" but there was no answer.

Orpheus could not bear to give up Eurydice for lost. After he had looked everywhere on earth, without finding her, he knew that she must be in the underworld. He made up his mind that he would go down and play before King Pluto. He thought perhaps he could persuade Pluto and Proserpine to let her come back to the sunny valley again.

So he went down into Pluto's kingdom, and there he played such a very sweet, sad song that tears came into the eyes of all who heard it. Even Pluto, whom men thought very hard-hearted, could not help feeling sorry for the singer.

When the song was over, Orpheus implored that Eurydice might be allowed to return with him to the upper world, saying that he could not return without her. Pluto consented to let her go on one condition, and that condition was, that Orpheus must have faith to believe that Eurydice was following him, and until he reached the upper air must not look back to see.

So Orpheus started back again, playing softly on

his lyre. The music was not sad now. You would have thought that the dawn was coming, and that young birds were just waking in their nests. In the darkness, for it is always dark in the underworld, Eurydice was following; but Orpheus could not be sure of this. He slowly climbed the steep path over the rocks, back to the world of light and warmth. Just as he had almost reached that familiar world; just as he could feel the fresh air from the sea on his forehead, and could see the glimmer of a sunbeam reflected on the rocks, he felt all at once as if Eurydice were not there. The thought flashed into his mind that King Pluto might be deceiving him. He turned his head, and by the dim light which was beginning to break over his path, saw Eurydice fading away and sinking down into the underworld. Her arms were stretched out toward him, but she could not follow him any farther. He had broken the condition imposed by Pluto, hence Eurydice must go back among the shades.

Oh, if only he had not looked back! Eurydice was lost indeed now. Orpheus knew that it would be of no use to try again to bring her to the upper world. He did not go back to the pleasant valley in which he had grown up, but went to live on a lonely mountain, where he spent all his days in grieving for Eurydice.

The music that came from his lyre was so sad,

now, that it would have broken any one's heart to hear it. When the wind blew from the north, the people who lived at the foot of the mountain could faintly hear the mournful, wailing sound of the lyre. It came down the mountain to them, almost every day, for seven months, and then the north wind did not bring them those strains any more. Some said that Orpheus had been killed by lightning, and others that he had been torn in pieces by the Mænads, certain wild, half-crazed women who wandered over that mountain; but no one ever knew what really did become of him.

His lyre floated down the river Hebrus, and then out to sea, sending out sweet sounds as it went, with the rise and fall of the water. One day, when the waves ran high, it was cast up on the shore at the island of Lesbos. There it remained till it was all overgrown with vines and flowers, and half-buried under falling leaves. The nightingales were said to sing more sweetly on that island than in any other place.

32

Ganymede

A SINGULARLY beautiful boy called Ganymede was
playing one day on the hills near Troy, when a great
black cloud suddenly overspread the sun and a sudden
wind sent the dust and the leaves flying. There was
a roll of thunder, with a few flashes of lightning, and
then an enormous black eagle suddenly swooped
down from the cloud, caught up Ganymede in its
talons, and sailed away.

Tros, Ganymede's father, who was in a neighbouring field, saw all that happened; but although he
shouted and ran and threw sticks and stones toward
the fast-rising bird, the eagle was far beyond the
reach of such missiles long before Tros arrived at the
hill where Ganymede had been playing.

So the poor father, overcome with grief, went
home and told his wife what had happened. When
the neighbours heard the story, they all gathered
together at the house of Tros and mourned with the
grief-stricken father and mother. It was of no use to
search for Ganymede, for the eagle had taken him
far beyond the mountains of that country.

A few days later a strange visitor came to the house of Tros. He carried a curious rod with snakes twined round it, and two shadowy wings fluttered from his cap. "Do not mourn for Ganymede," said he, "the boy has met with great good fortune. His beauty has caused him to be loved by Jupiter, who has taken him for his cup-bearer; he pours ruby nectar into a golden cup for the king of the gods; he will never die nor grow old."

When Tros heard these words, he was comforted.

33

The Bag of Winds

The island of King Æolus lay in the midst of the sea, very far away from any other land. Not being fixed in one place, like other islands, it floated slowly on the water. Exactly in the middle of it was a palace, or castle. A strong bronze wall, very steep and smooth, had been built all around the palace. Here, with his six sons and six daughters, lived Æolus, the king of the winds.

When Ulysses, who was the king of Ithaca, was coming home from the Trojan War, he lost his way. After a very long voyage, and a great many hardships, he came with his men, one day, to the floating island of King Æolus.

Here they were hospitably received. In fact, King Æolus kept them at his palace and entertained them for a month. When they were ready to start out again, on their way home, King Æolus gave Ulysses a great leather bag, made of an ox-skin, and tied with a silver rope. In this bag were all the winds except one. That one wind was the west wind, which King Æolus had purposely kept outside, so that it might blow the ship home; for Ithaca was toward the east.

When the sailors saw King Æolus hand over this great leather bag to Ulysses, they did not know what was in it, but thought it must be something very valuable, probably gold. Then noticing the shining silver rope with which it was bound, they began to wonder if they could not undo the knot.

Ulysses, seeing their curious glances, and feeling a little suspicious of them, made up his mind that he would sit up all night, every night, and steer the ship himself.

They started off, with the west wind blowing gently, and all going well. For nine days and nine nights they sailed straight east, till they could see the mountain peaks of Ithaca. All this time, Ulysses had been at the helm, for he felt more and more suspicious of the sailors.

Meanwhile, the sailors whispered among themselves that Ulysses was going home with a great bag of treasure, and that it was not fair that they should have nothing. They could see more and more of the shores of Ithaca. Even the smoke from their own firesides came in sight, and that was a sight they had not seen before for many long years.

But Ulysses could not keep awake any longer. When he saw land in sight, and knew that the voyage was almost over, he was so completely tired out that he sank down by the rudder where he stood, and fell asleep. This gave the sailors the opportunity they had been watching for. They sprang to the bag the moment that the eyes of Ulysses were closed, and untied the silver rope.

Out rushed the winds, and struck the ship from all ways at once. The ship spun around like a top, and the sea was churned into a fine spray which flew so high and so thick that it was like a blinding snowstorm. Then, being blown along by a gale from the east, Ulysses and his men finally found themselves once more at the Island of the Winds.

But as King Æolus would not help them a second time, they had to make the best of it, and take the winds as they came. It was a long, long time after that, before they saw their homes again.

34

Circe

I

THE PURPLE WOODPECKER

ONE day King Picus was in the forest near his palace, hunting wild boars. He was mounted on a very spirited black horse, and surrounded by his guards. Even when hunting he wore his crown and a purple robe, fastened with a gold buckle, for this king was rather fond of wearing fine clothes.

The forest was a beautiful place. It was full of great oaks, which grew so thick together that the sun could scarcely shine through their branches. The king was fond of riding, and liked to hunt in this forest; but he would have been wiser if he had taken his recreation somewhere else; for he had a dangerous neighbour that often frequented this place.

This was Circe, the famous enchantress. Very dreadful stories were told of her. She lived in a marble palace not so very far from the palace of King Picus, and she and the maids or nymphs who attended her, spent a great deal of their time roaming in the royal forest, searching for the poisonous plants which they used in their enchantments.

One day, at the very hour that King Picus was hunting in the forest, it happened that Circe and a few of her nymphs were among the oaks, looking for a plant from whose root Circe knew how to make a very powerful drug. They saw the king and his guards, and kept themselves concealed among the trees.

King Picus suddenly thought he saw a wild boar run in among the bushes. As the place was such a tangle of thorn-trees and thick-growing shrubs and prickly vines, that the king could not go any farther on horseback, he dismounted, intending to follow the beast on foot. He did not know that the wild boar was only a shadow, which Circe, by her enchantments, had caused him to see.

Circe, herself, was in the thicket, and before King Picus could get away, she touched him with her wand, changing him into a little purple woodpecker. His crown became a crest of feathers, and his gold buckle, a yellow ring encircling his neck.

When King Picus did not come back, his guards rode in all directions, looking for him. At last they saw Circe, and knowing how many wicked things she had already done, they feared she was the cause of the king's disappearance. They would have killed her on the spot with their javelins, but it suddenly grew so dark that they could see nothing, while a strong wind began to blow, and the great oak branches creaked overhead. Then, under cover of the darkness which she had called down, Circe struck the guards, in turn, with her wand, changing them from brave young men into different kinds of wild beasts. Here, far away from home and friends, they were obliged to live in the king's forest, sleeping under bushes and eating roots and berries. The little purple woodpecker beat his tattoo over their heads, but they did not know that this bird was really King Picus.

II

ULYSSES AT CIRCE'S PALACE

Not long after the time when King Picus and his guards met with such a sad misfortune in the oak forest, a ship sailed into the harbour near Circe's palace. In this ship were King Ulysses and his men— the same men who had let loose the winds which King Æolus had bound for them in a bag. Since the adventure with the bag of winds, they had met with some terrible hardships, and were reduced in number. They drew their galley up on the shore, and then lay down to sleep under the trees near by; for they were exhausted with hard rowing in the hot sun. Finding the place very comfortable, they remained there for two days.

On the third day they found that their supply of provisions was entirely gone. The men began to complain, and to blame King Ulysses, although they knew very well that they would all have been safe at home long ago, if they, themselves, had not meddled with the bag of winds.

It was plain that they must go farther inland if they wished to find any game; but not one of them cared to venture far from the place where the galley lay, as they did not know what dangers they might encounter.

At last, as none of the men were willing to go, King Ulysses himself took his hunting spear and started out alone. As he disappeared behind the trees, the men whispered to one another that this was quite right. Let him take the risk of exploring the island. Had they not spent their strength in rowing?

King Ulysses went to a high place, where he could look out over the entire island. He saw a slender column of black smoke going up from the midst of a dense thicket in the centre of the island. He believed that this indicated some human habitation, where his ship's company might hope for hospitality. He went quickly back to the ship with the news, and on his way succeeded in killing a fat buck, which made a good supper for himself and his men. His followers began to think that they had not such a bad leader, after all.

When the supper was over, Ulysses told about the smoke he had seen. It was agreed that the whole company should be divided into two parts, half the men in each, with a leader; that they should then draw lots; and that those to whom the lot fell should go to see what was to be found at the place where the smoke had been seen.

So Ulysses counted off the men, of whom there were forty-four in all. Over twenty-two of them he set his friend Eurylochus; the other twenty-two he commanded himself. Then he and Eurylochus shook pebbles in a bronze helmet, and the pebble of Eurylochus bounded from the helmet first. Eurylochus was willing to go, but the men he commanded thought themselves most cruelly used. They preferred to stay near the ship and wait for Ulysses to bring them another fat buck.

Early the next morning, when Eurylochus and his twenty-two men reached the thicket, they found a glade in the midst of it. In the glade stood a beautiful palace, built of white marble blocks which were so highly polished that they shone in the morning sun like diamonds.

As the party came near the palace, hundreds of wild beasts—lions and panthers, bears and wolves—sprang up from every point and came toward them. The men expected to be torn to pieces, but what was their surprise to see these savage creatures approach them in the most friendly way. The lions rubbed against them caressingly, and the wolves wagged their tails, like house-dogs. Upon this, the men plucked up their courage and went boldly up to the palace doors. Then they heard the whirring of a loom and the voice of a woman singing. These were such sounds as they might have heard in their own homes. So with growing confidence they shouted loudly, to let the people within the palace know that some one was there.

Presently a woman with beautiful golden hair opened the great doors wide and invited them to enter. Eurylochus, fearing that some trap might be laid for them, remained outside, but all the others went into the palace.

Each of the twenty-two men had lost all fear now. They were ushered into rooms more beautiful than any they had ever seen before, where tapestries of the richest colours hung on the walls and embroideries of exquisite fineness covered the couches and the chairs. Everything was as luxurious as possible. These chance travellers were treated like guests of honour. They were invited to seat themselves on the embroidered chairs, and were served with wine by four pretty maids. The wine had a most remarkable flavour, but the men were sure that this was nothing to what was coming, for now and then delightful whiffs reached them from the kitchen, where they had no doubt an appetizing repast was being prepared. All these things were exactly what they liked. Nothing could have suited them better. They were not sorry now that the lot had fallen to them, and as they drank their wine, they began to nudge one another and to laugh with pleasure at the thought of what Ulysses and the rest of the crew had lost.

Then, all at once, the gracious smiles of the beautiful lady with the golden hair changed to angry frowns, and she struck each of the men sharply with a long wand that she carried in her hand. The men tried to speak, but could only squeal, and in a moment more each of them saw his twenty-one companions changed to so many frightened swine, with bright little eyes, white bristles, and curly tails. They all jumped down from their embroidered chairs, and began to run wildly about the room, squealing with all their might, and upsetting the furniture in their efforts to escape. But Circe had them fast. She drove them to the sties with her wand, and scornfully threw them a few handfuls of acorns.

Eurylochus waited for a long time outside. At length, as the men did not come back, he returned to the ship, and told Ulysses that all the men were lost.

Ulysses immediately took his sword and his bow and started alone for the palace, to see what could be done. As he was passing through the oak forest, he met Mercury in his winged cap. This was most fortunate, because Mercury knew all about Circe and her enchantments.

"Where are you going, alone in this forest?" said Mercury.

"I am going to the palace in yonder glade, to seek my men," said Ulysses.

"That is the palace of Circe," said Mercury, "and the men you are seeking are penned up in Circe's sties, eating acorns. Is not that a very good place for them?" he added, with a twinkle in his eye. "They have made you trouble enough before now. You had better go home and leave them there."

Ulysses knew the faults of his men, but he would not think of leaving them to such a fate. "No," he said, "it was I who sent them to the palace. I must rescue them or share their misfortunes."

"Very well," said Mercury. "There is a flower whose virtue is stronger than any of Circe's enchantments." He began to look about him under the trees. Just then a handsome purple woodpecker flew past them, and began tapping on the trunk of an oak. Under this tree Mercury found the flower he wanted. It was a pure white flower with a black root. Mercury plucked it and handed it to Ulysses. "Take this flower," he said. "Be very careful not to lose it. As long as you have it with you, Circe can work you no harm. You may enter her palace if you wish. She will offer you wine in which she has placed a powerful drug. Drink it. It cannot hurt you. If she strikes at you with her wand, strike at her again with your sword. When she sees that her enchantments will not work, she will be afraid. You can then compel her to restore your men to their human shape."

When Mercury said this, the little purple woodpecker came fluttering down from the oak tree with a loud cry, and Mercury told Ulysses that this woodpecker was, in reality, King Picus, who had been transformed by Circe's arts into a bird with gay feathers, but who deserved to be changed into a king again. He also said that the lions, wolves, and other beasts that guarded Circe's gate were once men who, like King Picus, had been transformed by Circe.

Mercury, having told Ulysses all that was necessary, now went back to Olympus, while Ulysses, with the white flower in his hand, walked on through the forest, and soon reached the palace of Circe. The strange beasts came bounding out, and fawned on him as they had done on his companions. He called aloud at the palace doors, and Circe opened them wide. She took him into a splendid room, and invited him to be seated on a silver throne; for she knew that he was a king. She mixed wine for him in a golden cup, slyly putting in the magic drug.

Ulysses drank, without fear, believing in the power of the white flower. Then Circe struck at him fiercely with her wand. But Ulysses, instead of taking the form of some animal, stood up straight, looking more king-like than ever, and struck back at her with his sword.

Circe wrung her hands and fell on her knees, beseeching him to spare her. Ulysses made her promise that she would restore his men, and as many others as he should choose, to their proper human shape.

Then he went with her to the sties, and she sprinkled the twenty-two crowding, squealing swine with the juice of a certain plant, and there stood the companions of Ulysses, looking very much as they had done before they entered the palace of Circe.

They were beside themselves with happiness at being able to stand before the world like men again. Their strange experience made them see to what their selfish ways had been leading them, and from that day, when anything occurred which compelled them to choose between their own ease or pleasure and the good of others, they chose more wisely than they had ever done before.

The little purple woodpecker soon came fluttering around the head of Ulysses, who caused Circe to sprinkle the bird with the juice of the magic plant. Then once more the handsome King Picus, in his purple robes, stood before them. After this, the former guards of King Picus were restored to their human shape, with such other of the beasts about Circe's palace as deserved that kindness. But some of the cruel tigers and wolves were left as they were, to snarl and howl in the shape which best befitted their savage natures.

35

Arion and the Dolphin

ARION was a wonderful poet, who sang his own poems to the accompaniment of the lyre. His home was on the island of Lesbos, off the coast of Asia Minor. He was seldom to be found at home, however, for he wandered about, from one country to another, singing at the courts of kings.

At that time there were many other poets who sang their own songs, but not one could compare with Arion.

When he sang at the court of Corinth, the king's hunting dogs used to come bounding in to listen to the music, as much pleased as the courtiers. If he sang in the evening, with the doors open for coolness, fierce wolves used to come down from the hills in the darkness and gather around the palace, eager to hear the bewitching sound of the lyre. One could see their eyes shine just outside the doors, but the moment the music ceased they were gone. Overhead, great owls came flapping into the dark trees, and there were other listeners, too, of which the people of the court knew nothing.

One day the news reached Corinth that a musical

contest was to be held in Sicily, at which a bag of gold was to be the prize. All the poets of Greece meant to go—not so much for the gold as for the glory that they hoped to gain there.

Arion did not care greatly either for the gold or the glory, but he loved singing better than anything else in the world, and he liked to see new countries. Therefore he said he would go, too, but promised to return to Corinth when the contest was over.

The king of Sicily and the judges were very much surprised when they heard Arion's extraordinary playing, and they awarded him the prize without any question. They would have been glad to keep him in Sicily, but Arion, remembering his promise to the king of Corinth, engaged a Corinthian ship to take him back to that city.

The sun never seemed brighter, nor the sea bluer, than it did on the day when Arion started out to return to Corinth with his prize. Soon Sicily was out of sight, all but her mountains, which still showed faintly against the horizon. Arion was watching the disappearance of the last peak, when suddenly he found himself surrounded by the sailors, all armed. He understood at once that they had conspired against him, in order to obtain possession of the gold. The captain stepped up to him with an unsheathed sword in his hand, and said, "Give me that bag of gold you carry, and prepare to die!"

"But if I give you the gold, will you not let me
live?" said Arion.

"No, you must die!" answered the hard-hearted
captain, for he was afraid that if he let Arion live, the
king of Corinth might find out what had happened.

"I am not afraid to die," said Arion, "but give me
leave to sing one last song to my harp."

"That you may do," said the captain; "but when
the song is finished, you must throw yourself into
the sea."

Then the captain and the sailors retired to the
middle of the vessel, not unwilling to hear so famous
a singer, while Arion, in his court dress, stood up on
the stern, looking sadly toward the beautiful island
of Sicily, and sang one last song.

The singer's voice floated out over the water, and
a school of dolphins, swimming by just then, heard
it, and came leaping after the ship.

When the song was over, Arion, with the lyre still
in his hands, leaped straight down into the sea.
Then the sailors sprang to the oars, and rowed as
fast as they could, making all possible haste to leave
the spot where they had done such a wicked deed.

But a wise old dolphin, who had come up to listen
to the music, saw Arion leap from the stern of the
ship, and caught the musician on his back. Then he
set out to swim to Corinth with him.

As Arion rode on the wise dolphin's back, with

the other dolphins leaping along behind, he played on his lyre, and the little waves were so charmed that they grew still, to listen. So the procession reached Corinth in safety.

The king was greatly astonished, and could not believe what Arion told him. As soon as the wicked sailors arrived, he sent for them and asked them what had become of Arion.

"He is well and happy," said they, "but has made up his mind that he will remain in Italy."

The king then sent for Arion, who came in wearing the same court dress in which he had leaped into the sea. The sailors were so taken by surprise that they confessed everything, and the king banished them from the country. But Arion was the greatest hero in all Greece.

36

Psyche

I

THE PALACE OF EROS

A CERTAIN king had three daughters who were known far and wide for their beauty. The most beautiful of all was the youngest, Psyche. When this youngest princess went into the temples, many people mistook her for Venus herself, and offered her the garlands which they had brought for the goddess of love and beauty.

The real Venus, much vexed by this, determined to be revenged on poor Psyche, who was in no way to blame. One day she told Eros, the god of love, to wound Psyche with one of his golden-pointed arrows, and make her fall in love with some wretched beggar, the most degraded that could be found.

Eros took his arrows and went down to the earth to do his mother's bidding. As soon as he saw Psyche, he was so startled by her wonderful beauty that he wounded himself with his own arrow; consequently, instead of making Psyche fall in love with some ragged beggar, he himself fell in love with Psyche.

Long before this the two elder of the three beautiful sisters had been married to kings' sons, as befitted the rank of princesses; but in spite of her superior beauty, no lovers came to sue for the hand of the youngest sister. The king, suspecting that this might be caused by the wrath of Venus, inquired of the oracle what he should do. The answer that he received allowed him no longer to doubt the anger of the gods. These were the words of the prophetess:

Dress thy daughter like a bride,
Lead her up the mountain-side,
There an unknown wingèd foe,
Feared by all who dwell below,
And even by the gods above,
Will claim her, as a hawk the dove.

The king was overcome with grief, but did not dare to disobey. Therefore one night Psyche's maids of honour dressed her in wedding garments, and a long procession of her father's people escorted her to an exposed rock at the top of a high mountain, where they sadly extinguished their torches, and left her alone in the darkness.

After the last sound of human footsteps had died away, Psyche sat weeping and trembling, fearing every moment that she might hear the rushing wings of some dragon, and feel his claws and teeth. Instead, she felt the cool breath and the downy wings of Zephyrus, the west wind, who lifted her gently from the rock, then puffed out his cheeks, and blew her down into a beautiful green valley, where he laid her softly on a bank of violets.

This moonlit valley was so sweet and peaceful that Psyche forgot her fears and fell asleep. When she woke in the morning, she saw a beautiful grove of tall trees, and in the grove a most wonderful palace, with a fountain in front of it. The great arches of the roof were supported by golden columns, and the walls were covered with silver carving, while the floor was a mosaic of precious stones of all colours.

Psyche timidly entered the doors, and wandered through the great rooms, each of which seemed more splendid than the last. She could see no one, but once or twice thought she heard low voices, as if the fairies were talking together. It might have been voices, or it might have been the trickling of water in the fountain.

Presently, she opened the door of a room, where a table was laid ready for a feast. Evidently only one guest was expected, for there was but one chair and one cover. Psyche, half afraid, seated herself in the chair, and the fairies of the palace, or the nymphs, or whatever beings the voices belonged to, came and waited on her, but not one of them could be seen. She enjoyed a most appetizing repast. After the last dish had been whisked away by invisible hands, she heard music—a chorus of singing voices, and then a single voice, accompanied by a lyre, which seemed to play of itself.

As the light faded away, and night came, Psyche began to tremble, for she feared that the owner of the palace might prove to be the winged monster of the oracle, and that he would come to claim her. There were no locks nor bolts, and the doors and windows stood wide open, as if no thief, nor evil creature of any kind, had ever lived.

When it had grown perfectly dark, so dark that she could not see her own hand, Psyche heard the sound of wings, and then footsteps coming down the great hall. The footsteps came lightly and quickly to the low seat where she was sitting, and then a voice which was sweet and musical said to her: "Beautiful Psyche, this palace and all it holds is yours, if you will consent to live here and be my wife. The voices you have heard are the voices of your hand-maidens, who will obey any commands that you give them. Every night I will spend here with you; but before day comes, I must fly away. Do not ask to see my face, nor to know who I am. Only trust me; I ask nothing more."

This speech took away Psyche's fear of being immediately eaten, at any rate; but still she could not be quite sure that this voice was not the voice of the monster.

Her mysterious lover came to talk to her every

night, as he had said he would do. Sometimes she looked forward to his coming with pleasure; at other times the sound of his wings filled her with terror.

One day, while she was gathering roses within sight of the rock from which Zephyrus had blown her into the valley, she saw her two sisters on this rock, weeping, beating their breasts, and crying out as if mourning for the dead. Hearing her own name, she knew that her sisters must be mourning for her, supposing that she had been devoured on this rock. These sisters of Psyche had not always been kind to her; but she now believed that they had really loved her after all.

That night, when her lover came in the dark, Psyche asked him if she might not see her sisters, and let them know that she was alive and happy. She received an unwilling consent.

The next day the sisters came again to the high rock, and Zephyrus blew them down into the valley, just as he had blown Psyche down. They were very much surprised to see the good fortune that had befallen their little sister; but instead of rejoicing at it, as they should have done, they were envious of her. They asked her a great many questions, and were particularly curious about the owner of the palace. Psyche told them that he was away hunting on the mountains. Then Zephyrus, thinking that they were getting too inquisitive, whisked them away to the rock, and that was the end of their visit.

After a time Psyche grew tired of being so much alone, and wished to see her sisters again. Her lover gave his consent a second time, but warned her not to answer or even to listen to any questions about himself, and told her, above all, that if she ever tried to see him face to face, he should be forced to fly away and leave her, and that the palace also would vanish.

The next day Zephyrus brought the sisters into the valley as before. These envious women had brooded over their sister's superior fortune till their minds were full of wicked thoughts, and between them they made a plan by which they meant to destroy Psyche's happiness. They told her that the owner of the palace was, without doubt, a most horrible winged serpent, the nameless monster of the oracle, and that the people who lived on the mountain had seen him coming down into that valley, every day toward dusk. "Although he seems so kind," said they, "he is only waiting his time to devour you. He knows that you would be terrified by his ugly scales, and this is the reason he never allows you to see him. But listen to the advice of your sisters, who are older and wiser than you. Take this knife, and while your pretended friend is asleep, light a lamp and look at him. If our words prove to be true, strike off his head, and save yourself from an awful death."

With these words her sisters left Psyche the knife and hurried away. When they had gone, poor Psyche could not rid her mind of the fears their words had raised. Her faith was gone. If all were right, why was her lover so anxious to be hidden in the darkness? Why did he fear her sisters' visits? Why did he have wings? Worst of all, she remembered, with a shudder, that she had once or twice heard a sound like the gliding of a serpent over the marble floors.

Soon it grew dark, and she heard her lover coming. That night she would not talk to him, therefore he went into a chamber where there was a couch, lay down and fell asleep.

Then Psyche, trembling with fear, lighted her lamp, took the knife, and stole to the couch where he lay. The light of the lamp fell full on his face, and Psyche saw no scaly serpent, but Eros, or Love himself, the most beautiful of the gods. Golden curls fell back from his wonderful face; his snow-white wings were folded in sleep, while the down on them—as delicate as that on the wings of a butterfly—stirred faintly, set in motion by his quiet breathing. At his feet lay his bow and arrows.

Psyche dropped her knife, in horror at the deed it might have done. Then taking up an arrow curiously, she pricked her finger on its golden point. Holding her lamp high above her head, she turned to look at Eros again, and now for the first time in love with Love, gazed at him in an ecstasy of happiness; but her hand trembled, and a drop of hot oil fell on the shoulder of the god. He opened his eyes, looked at her reproachfully, and then flew away without a word. The beautiful palace vanished, and Psyche found herself alone.

II

THE TRIAL OF PSYCHE

Then Psyche began a long search for her lost Eros. She met Pan, Ceres, and Juno, one after another, but none of them could help her. At last she went to Venus herself, thinking that the mother of Love would be kind to her for Love's sake.

Eros, at this time, lay in the palace of Venus, suffering from the wound caused by the burning oil. Venus knew all that had happened, for a gull had flown to her and told her. She was very angry, and as a punishment imposed certain almost impossible tasks upon Psyche.

First, the goddess pointed to a great heap of seeds, the food of the doves that drew her chariot, and of the little sparrows that accompanied her on her journeys. It was composed of wheat, barley, millet, and other kinds of seed, all mixed carelessly together.

"Take these," said Venus, "and separate them grain by grain; place each kind by itself, and finish the task before nightfall."

Poor Psyche had no courage to begin the task, but sat with drooping head and folded hands. Then a little ant ran out from under a stone, and called the whole army of the ant people, who came for Love's sake, and quickly separated the seeds, laying each kind by itself.

When Venus came at the close of the day, and saw that Psyche's task was finished, she was very much surprised, and throwing the poor girl a piece of coarse bread, remarked that a harder task would be set for her in the morning. Accordingly, when morning came, Venus took Psyche to the bank of a broad river, and pointing to a grove on the opposite shore, where a flock of sheep with golden wool were feeding, said, "Bring me some of that wool."

Psyche would have plunged immediately into the river, if some reeds on the bank had not whispered to her: "Do not go near those sheep now. They are fierce creatures when the sun is high. Wait till the song of the river has lulled them to sleep; then go and pick all the wool you like from the bushes, where the sheep have left it clinging." So Psyche waited till the sun was low, then crossed the river and came back with her arms full of golden wool.

Venus, seeing Psyche return in safety, was angrier

than ever. "You never did this by yourself," said she. "Now we will see whether you are wise and prudent enough to become the bride of Eros. Take this crystal vase, and fill it with water from the Fountain of Forgetfulness."

This fountain was at the very top of a high mountain. The icy water gushed forth from a smooth rock, far higher than any one could climb, and as it rushed down its narrow channel it shouted, "Fly from me! Beware! Thou wilt perish!" On either side of the black stream was a cave, and in each cave lived a fierce dragon. When Psyche came to the place and saw all this, she was so horrified that she could not move or speak. Nevertheless, she accomplished this task also; for Jupiter's eagle, to whom Love had been kind, took the crystal vase and filled it for her at the fountain.

Psyche ran back to Venus with the water, hoping to please her this time. But Venus was still angry. "You are a witch," said she, "or you could not do these things. However, here is one task more. Take this box, carry it down into the underworld, and ask Proserpine if you may not bring back to me some of her beauty."

When Psyche heard this, she felt sure that Venus meant to destroy her, and thinking that it was of no use to struggle longer against the persecutions of the goddess, she climbed up the stairway of a lofty tower, intending to throw herself down from the top. But the stones of the tower cried out to her: "Listen, Psyche! From yonder dark chasm, choked with thorns, a path leads down to the underworld. Take a piece of barley-bread in each hand, and two pieces of money in your mouth, then follow this rough path. When you come to the river of the dead, Charon will ferry you over for one of your pieces of money. When you reach the gate of Pluto's palace, where Cerberus keeps watch, give that fierce dog one of the pieces of bread, and he will let you pass. You can then enter the palace where Proserpine is queen. She will give you a portion of her beauty, shutting it into the box, and you can return by the same way, giving the remaining piece of bread to Cerberus, and the remaining piece of money to Charon. One thing more. I charge you, do not, by any means, look into the box."

Psyche was thankful indeed for this advice, and followed it in every particular but one. When she was returning, she forgot the warning about not looking into the box. Since Love had flown away from her, her suffering had been so great that her beauty was nearly gone. Therefore, thinking that it might not be wrong to take a very little of Proserpine's beauty for herself, she raised the lid of the box. Whiff! A strange invisible something rushed from it and overcame her. She fell into a deep sleep, and might never have waked again if Love, cured of his wounds, had not passed by and seen her. The god shook her till she was awake again, then sent her back to his mother with the box, while he flew straight to Mount Olympus, and laid the case before Jupiter.

The king of the gods, after hearing the story, said that Psyche should be made immortal, and should become the bride of Eros.

Mercury was immediately sent to bring Psyche up to Mount Olympus, while the gods all gathered to a great feast. Jupiter himself handed to this mortal maid the cup of sacred nectar, of which whoever drinks will live forever. Psyche drank from the golden cup, and straightway two beautiful butterfly-like wings sprang from her shoulders, and she became like the gods in all things.

After this, she was wedded to Eros, who never flew away from her again. Apollo sang, and Venus, her anger forgotten, danced at the wedding.

Pronouncing and Explanatory Index

243

Athene (a thē'ne), or Athena (a thē'na). See *Minerva*

Atlas (at'las). A Titan who held up the sky, or, according to later accounts, the world, 18, 85, 180

Augean stables (â je'an). The stables of King Augeas, 168

Augeas (â'je as). A king of Elis, 169

Aurora (â rō'ra). [Gr. *Eos*.] The goddess of the dawn, 131

Bacchus (bak'kus). [Gr. *Dionysus*.] The god of the vine, 15, 138, 197

Baucis (bâ'sis). The wife of Philemon, 199

Bellerophon (bel ler'o fon). The hero who slew the Chimæra, 125

Boreas (bō're as). The north wind, 105

Briareus (briā're us). A giant with a hundred arms, 18

Cadmus (kad'mus). A prince of Phenicia, said to be the founder of Thebes, 64

caduceus (ka dū'se us). The wand or staff carried by Mercury, 15, 35, 38

Castor and Pollux (kas'tor and pol'-uks). The twin brothers of Helen, 104

Caucasian Mountains (kâ kā'shan). A mountain system between the Black and Caspian seas, 20, 173

centaur (sen'târ). A creature, half man and half horse, supposed to inhabit the mountains of Thessaly, 100, 163, 184

Cepheus (sē'fūs). The father of Andromeda, 86

Cerberus (sēr'be rus). The watch-dog at the gates of Hades, 181, 240

Ceres (sē'rēz). [Gr. *Demeter*.] The goddess of vegetation, 15, 40, 145

Ceyx (sē'iks). A king of Thessaly, 150

Charon (kā'ron). The boatman who ferried the souls of the dead over the rivers of the underworld, 240

Chimæra (kĭ mē'ra). A fire-breathing monster slain by Bellerophon, 125

Chiron (kī'ron). A centaur, the teacher of many of the Greek heroes, 100

cicada (si kā'da). The locust, 39

Cilix (sī'lix). The brother of Cadmus, 64

Circe (sēr'sē). An enchantress, the daughter of Helios, 215

Clytie (klī'tē). A nymph who loved the sun-god, and was changed into a flower, 56

Colchis (kol'kis). A country lying between the Caucasus and the Black Sea, 103, 118

Comatas (kō mā'tas). A shepherd, 123

Corinth (kor'inth). A city in Argolis, 229

Crete (krēt). An island in the Mediterranean, 168, 191

Cupid (kū'pid). The Roman god of love, 30

Dædalus (ded'a lus). A famous artisan of Crete, 195

Danaë (dan'a ē). The mother of Perseus, 76

Daphne (daf'ne). A nymph loved by Apollo, and changed into a laurel tree, 30

Deianeira (dē ya nī'ra). The wife of Hercules, 184